Body Language

FOR
DUMMIES®

PORTABLE EDITION

by Elizabeth Kuhnke

WILEY

A John Wiley and Sons, Ltd, Publication

Body Language For Dummies,® Portable Edition

Published by
John Wiley & Sons, Ltd
The Atrium
Southern Gate
Chichester
West Sussex
PO19 8SQ
England
www.wiley.com

For general information on our other products and services, please contact our Customer Care Department within the U.S. at 877-762-2974, outside the U.S. at 317-572-3993, or fax 317-572-4002.

For technical support, please visit www.wiley.com/techsupport.

Wiley publishes in a variety of print and electronic formats and by print-on-demand. Some material included with standard print versions of this book may not be included in e-books or in print-on-demand. If this book refers to media such as a CD or DVD that is not included in the version you pur-chased, you may download this material at http://booksupport.wiley.com. For more information about Wiley products, visit www.wiley.com.

British Library Cataloguing in Publication Data: A catalogue record for this book is available from the British Library

ISBN: 978-1-119-94556-7 (pbk); 978-1-119-94003-6 (ebk); 978-1-119-94004-3 (ebk); 978-1-119-94005-0 (ebk)

Printed and bound in Great Britain by TJ International, Padstow.

10 9 8 7 6 5 4 3

About the Author

Elizabeth Kuhnke is an international conference speaker, best-selling author and qualified coach who aims to provide her clients with the skills and knowledge to live the lives they envision, and make the changes they desire. Her clients and colleagues call her 'Diamond Polisher' because of her ability to smooth, sharpen and shape talented individuals, enabling them to reveal their true brilliance. Her three-pronged approach to client development is based on demonstrating respect, establishing rapport, and producing results. She believes that dogged determination combined with a healthy dose of fun are vital for success.

For over twenty years, Elizabeth has nourished a steady client stream of FTSE 100 companies, professional services and charities, providing one-to-one and group coaching in key areas relating to interpersonal communication including personal impact, confidence and influencing skills. Elizabeth's combination of advanced degrees, a career in the performing arts, expertise in administering psychometric instruments and a passion for personal best are some of the reasons clients turn to her for support.

She's been compared to an Olympic athlete, who never gives up. She has been equated to a pit bull because she never lets go. And she has been likened to a radiator, because she generates warmth. She is often quoted in the media addressing issues concerning confidence, persuasion and influence, voice, body language and public speaking skills.

Elizabeth is currently working on the second edition of *Body Language For Dummies*, and has also written *Persuasion & Influence For Dummies*. Contact Elizabeth through her website at www.kuhnkecommunication.com.

Author's Acknowledgments

Without friends, family, clients, and colleagues encouraging, nurturing, and spurring me along, this book would not now be in your hands. Allow me, if you will, to acknowledge but a small sampling of the support team.

The Author's Angels: Kate Burton, my buddy and fellow *For Dummies* author who believed I was the person for the job; Alison Yates who stuck with me when lesser mortals would have tossed in the towel; and Rachael Chilvers, whose marvellous cheerios brightened many a dark and dreary day.

Shaun Todd. An extraordinary coach and valued colleague.

Caroline Beery and Maria Jicheva who opened my eyes to diversity.

Neil Ginger and Jean Roberts for photos and fun.

All of my clients. You're stars. Keep breathing.

Toby Blundell who keeps me on track and makes me laugh.

Karl, Max, and Kristina. My joys.

Henry, ever faithful, always there.

As for the rest of the gang, you'll find yourselves within these pages. I am blessed to know you all.

Publisher's Acknowledgments

We're proud of this book; please send us your comments at http://dummies.custhelp.com. For other comments, please contact our Customer Care Department within the U.S. at 877-762-2974, outside the U.S. at 317-572-3993, or fax 317-572-4002.

Some of the people who helped bring this book to market include the following:

Acquisitions, Editorial, and Vertical Websites

Project Editor: Rachael Chilvers

Commissioning Editor: Alison Yates

Assistant Editor: Ben Kemble

Development Editor: Tracy Barr

Copy Editor: Anne O'Rorke

Technical Editor: Dr Peter Bull

Proofreader: Andy Finch

Production Manager: Daniel Mersey

Publisher: David Palmer

Cover Photos: © iStock/Daniel Laflor

Cartoons: Rich Tennant

Composition Services

Project Coordinator: Kristie Rees

Layout and Graphics: Christin Swinford

Indexer: Potomac Indexing, LLC

Publishing and Editorial for Consumer Dummies

Kathleen Nebenhaus, Vice President and Executive Publisher

Kristin Ferguson-Wagstaffe, Product Development Director

Ensley Eikenburg, Associate Publisher, Travel

Kelly Regan, Editorial Director, Travel

Publishing for Technology Dummies

Andy Cummings, Vice President and Publisher

Composition Services

Debbie Stailey, Director of Composition Services

Contents at a Glance

Table of Contents

Introduction

● ●

*B*ody language speaks louder than any words you can ever utter. Whether you're telling people that you love them, you're angry with them, or don't care less about them, your body movements reveal your thoughts, moods, and attitudes. Both consciously and sub-consciously your body tells observers what's really going on with you.

In a competitive and complex world the ability to communicate with clarity, confidence, and credibility is vital for success. Too frequently this ability is overlooked. Sound reasoning, logical conclusions and innovative solutions are rendered meaningless if they are not communicated in a way that persuades, motivates, and inspires the listener.

All day every day your body is relaying messages about your attitude, your mood, and your general state of being. You can determine what messages you relay by the way you use your body.

Although body language began with our ancient ancestors and long before vocal sounds turned into sophisticated words, phrases, and paragraphs, only in the last 60 years or so has body language been seriously studied. During that time people have come to appreciate the value of body language as a tool for enhancing interpersonal communication. Politicians, actors, and high-profile individuals recognise the part that their bodies play in conveying their messages.

Each chapter of this book addresses a specific aspect of body language. In addition to focusing on individual body parts and the role they play in communicating your thoughts, feelings, and attitudes, you discover how to interpret other people's body language, giving you an insight into their mental state before they may be aware of it themselves. Remember that you need to read body language in clusters and context. One gesture doesn't a story tell any more than does one word.

By performing specific actions and gestures, you can create corresponding mental states. By practising the gestures, you experience the positive impact of body language and discover how to create the image you want. You may actually become the person you want to be.

Are you ready? Read on.

About This Book

For a subject that's relatively new to the study of evolution and social behaviour, a tremendous amount of research has been done on body language. The impact of culture, gender, and religious differences on body language could each have a book devoted to them! I've written this book from a mostly English-speaking western perspective – much more could be written about body language in a cross-cultural communication context. However, I've been selective in what I've chosen to include and focused on using body language to improve your non-verbal communication for your personal and business relationships.

In this book I explain ways of recognising and identifying specific gestures, actions, and expressions that convey and support both the spoken and non-spoken message. By improving your reading of body language, understanding how your body conveys messages, and recognising how mood and attitude are reflected in your gestures and expressions, you have the upper hand in your interpersonal communications. By recognising and responding to body signals you can direct the flow of the conversation and facilitate meetings easily and effectively. I show you how your thoughts and feelings impact your gestures and expressions and how the same is true for others.

The point of the book is for you to become conscious of body language, both your own and other people's. It's also intended to aid you in correctly interpreting gestures, movements, and expressions. Finally, this book augments and develops the signs and signals you send out to enhance your communication.

Conventions Used in This Book

This book is a jargon-free zone. When I introduce a new term, I *italicise* it and then define it. The only other conventions in this book are that Web and e-mail addresses are in monofont, and the action part of numbered steps and the key concepts in a list are in **bold**. I alternate between using female and male pronouns in odd- and even-numbered chapters to be fair to both!

Foolish Assumptions

I assume, perhaps wrongly, that you:

- ✔ Are interested in body language and know a little bit about it
- ✔ Want to improve your interpersonal communications
- ✔ Are willing to reflect and respond
- ✔ Expect the best

How This Book is Organised

The cool thing about the *For Dummies* books is that you can dip in and out as you please. You don't need to read the first chapter to understand the last and if you read the last chapter first you won't ruin the story. The table of contents and index can help you find what you need. If you prefer to just dive in, please do – there's water in the pool. Read on for what lies ahead.

Part 1: In the Beginning was the Gesture

In this part I explore the foundations of body language, the silent communicator. You discover the origins of body language, how it evolved, and the impact it has on all your communications and relationships.

Part II: Starting at the Top

Focusing on the head and its parts and positions, I continue exploring body language and the messages it conveys. You discover how the tilt of your head and the lift of your brow reveal more than the words that tumble from your mouth.

Part III: The Trunk: Limbs and Roots

In this part I explore the impact of your posture on your thinking, attitudes, and perceptions. You see how feelings, behaviour, and perceptions are intertwined. I look at the body's limbs, its arms, legs, feet, hands, and fingers, and how their movements reflect inner states and create impressions.

Part IV: Putting the Body Into Social and Business Context

In this part you discover how to gesture effectively and appropriately according to the situation you're in. You find out where to place and position yourself for greatest effect. You discover how to read and reveal signs of interest and dismissal and how to engage with a possible romantic partner.

Addressing cultural diversity you get a glimpse into behaviours different from your own and pick up adaptive strategies for avoiding potential pitfalls.

Part V: The Part of Tens

If you're keen to get a handle on body language quickly and concisely, start with Part V. For developing your skills as a silent communicator and honing your observation skills, this is the place to be.

Icons Used in This Book

For sharpening your thinking and focusing your attention, let these icons be your guide.

 This icon highlights stories to entertain and inform you about friends of mine, or people I've seen, and the clues they've revealed through body language.

 Here's a chance for you to stand back and observe without being seen. By distancing yourself and taking a bird's eye view you can watch how others behave and reflect on the outcome.

 This icon underscores a valuable point to keep in mind.

 These are practical and immediate remedies for honing your body language skills.

 Here you can have a go at putting theory into practice. Some of the practical exercises are designed to enhance your image and create an impact.

Where to Go from Here

Although all the material in this book is designed to support you in being yourself at your best, not all the information may be pertinent to your specific needs or interests. Read what you want, when you want. You don't have to read the book in order, nor is there a sell by date for covering the material.

If you're interested in how body language conveys messages, begin with Part I. If you're seeking to improve your body language for a first date, have a look at Chapter 11. If you're curious about facial expressions have a look at Chapter 4.

Now, flip to a page, chapter, or section that interests you and read away. Feel free to dip and dive from section to section and page to page. Most importantly, enjoy the read.

Part I
In the Beginning was the Gesture

The 5th Wave   By Rich Tennant

"I assume that means either 'rub my feet,' or 'find my socks.' Any other meaning will require a spoken word or another body part."

In this part . . .

*H*ere's where we explore the foundations of body language, the way of silently communicating that can improve your impact factor and relationships once you grasp even the basics. In this part we go back in time to the origins of body language, how it's evolved, and its subtle power.

Chapter 1

Defining Body Language

• •

In This Chapter

▶ Finding out how body language speaks for you

▶ Gesturing for a purpose

▶ Understanding what you're communicating

• •

*T*he science of body language is a fairly recent study, dating primarily from around 60 years ago, although body language itself is, of course, as old as humans. Psychologists, zoologists, and social anthropologists have conducted detailed research into the components of body language – part of the larger family known as non-verbal behaviour.

If you're quiet for a moment and take the time to pay attention to body language movements and expressions that silently communicate messages of their own, you can cue in on gestures that convey a feeling and transmit a thought. If you pay close attention, you can identify gestures that you automatically associate with another person, which tell you who she is. In addition, you may notice other types of gestures that reveal a person's inner state at that moment.

In this chapter you discover how to interpret non-verbal language, exploring the gestures and actions that reveal thoughts, attitudes, and emotions. Also, you have a quick glance at some of the research into this unspoken language and recognise similarities and differences throughout the world. In addition, you find out how you can use gestures to enhance your relationships and improve your communication.

Discovering How Body Language Conveys Messages

When cave-dwellers discovered how to decipher grunts and to create words to convey their message, their lives became a lot more complex. Before verbal communication, they relied on their bodies to communicate. Their simple brains informed their faces, torsos, and limbs. They instinctively knew that fear, surprise, love, hunger, and annoyance were different attitudes requiring different gestures. Emotions were less complex then, and so were the gestures.

Speech is a relatively new introduction to the communication process and is mainly used to convey information, including facts and data. Body language, on the other hand, has been around forever. Without relying on the spoken word for confirmation, the body's movements convey feelings, attitudes, and emotions. Like it or not, your body language, or non-verbal behaviour, says more about you, your attitudes, moods, and emotions, than you may want to reveal.

According to research conducted by Professor Albert Mehrabian of the University of California, Los Angeles, 55 per cent of the emotional message in face-to-face communication results from body language. You only have to experience any of the following gestures or expressions to know how true the expression is, 'Actions speak louder than words':

- ✔ Someone pointing her finger at you
- ✔ A warm embrace
- ✔ A finger wagging in your face
- ✔ A child's pout
- ✔ A lover's frown
- ✔ A parent's look of worry
- ✔ An exuberant smile
- ✔ Your hand placed over your heart

Projecting an image in the first 30 seconds

You can tell within the first seven seconds of meeting someone how she feels about herself by the expression on her face and the way she moves her body. Whether she knows it or not, she's transmitting messages through her gestures and actions.

You walk into a room of strangers and from their stance, movements, and expressions you receive messages about their feelings, moods, attitudes, and emotions. Look at the teenage girl standing in the corner. From her slouching shoulders, her lowered head, and the way her hands fidget over her stomach, you can tell that this little wallflower is lacking in self-confidence.

Another young woman in this room of strangers is standing in a group of contemporaries. She throws her head back as she laughs, her hands and arms move freely and openly, and her feet are planted firmly beneath her, hip width apart. This woman is projecting an image of self-confidence and joie de vivre that draws people to her.

How you position your head, shoulders, torso, arms, hands, legs, and feet, and how your eyes, mouth, fingers, and toes move, tell an observer more about your state of being, including your attitude, emotions, thoughts, and feelings, than any words you can say.

Transmitting messages unconsciously

Although you're capable of choosing gestures and actions to convey a particular message, your body also sends out signals without your conscious awareness. Dilated or contracted eye pupils and the unconscious movements of your hands and feet are examples of signals that reveal an inner emotion that the person signalling may prefer to conceal. For example, if you notice that the pupils of someone's eyes are dilated, and you know that she's not under the influence of drugs, you'd be correct in assuming that whatever she's looking at is giving her pleasure. If the pupils are contracted the opposite is true. These individual signals can be easily overlooked or misidentified if they're taken out of their social context, or if they're not identified as part of a cluster of gestures involving other parts of the body.

At times in life you may want to conceal your thoughts and feelings, so you behave in a way that you believe hides what's going on inside. And yet wouldn't you know it, out pops a slight giveaway gesture, often invisible to the untrained eye, sending a signal that all's not what it appears. Just because these micro gestures and expressions are fleeting doesn't mean that they're not powerful.

In the 1970s, Paul Ekman and W V Friesen developed the Facial Action Coding System (FACS) to measure, describe, and interpret facial behaviours. This instrument is designed to measure even the slightest facial muscle contractions and determine what category or categories each facial action fits into. It can detect what the naked eye can't and is used by law enforcement agencies, film animators, and researches of human behaviour.

University of California, Los Angeles (UCLA) Professor Albert Mehrabian's classic study of how messages are received and responded to during face-to-face communication shows that when an incongruity exists between the spoken word and how you deliver it, 7 per cent of the message is conveyed through your words, 38 per cent is revealed through your vocal quality, and a whopping 55 per cent of your message comes through your gestures, expression, and posture. Mehrabian's premise is that the way people communicate is inseparable from the feelings that they project, consciously or not, in daily social interactions. Although some people contest Mehrabian's figures, the point remains that body language and vocal quality significantly contribute to the meaning of the message and determine the effectiveness of our relationships.

Arthur is the chief executive of a global telecoms company. Highly accomplished and rewarded for his successes, he still harbours some self-doubt and insecurity. This uncertainty is particularly evident when he's making formal presentations. He holds a pad of paper in front of himself, as if it were a protective shield. When he's unsure of the word he wants to use, he quickly and briefly rubs the skin under his nose with his index finger. When he moves from one point to the next in his presentation, he quickly taps his forehead with his left index finger as if to remind himself that he's about to move to the next point. Seeing himself on DVD he recognised how these meaningless gestures were revealing his lack of security, and how uncomfortable he feels in front of a large audience. By visualising himself presenting at his best and modelling specific behaviours of presenters who Arthur thinks are excellent, he developed ways of eliminating his unconscious negative gestures.

Substituting behaviour for the spoken word

Sometimes a gesture is more effective in conveying a message than any words you can use. Signals expressing love and support, pleasure and pain, fear, loathing, and disappointment are clear to decipher and require few, if any, words for clarification. Approval, complicity, or insults are commonly communicated without a sound passing between lips. By frowning, smiling, or turning your back on another person, your gestures need no words to clarify their meaning.

When words aren't enough or the word mustn't be spoken out loud, you gesture to convey your meaning. Some examples are

- ✔ Putting your index finger in front of your mouth while at the same time pursing your lips is a common signal for silence.

- ✔ Putting your hand up sharply with your fingers held tightly together and your palm facing forward means 'Stop!'.

- ✔ Winking at another person hints at a little secret between the two of you.

When Libby, the well loved and highly successful Artistic Director of the Oregon Shakespeare Festival was honoured for her years of service, she felt proud and humbled. Looking around the room filled with colleagues, friends, and major financial contributors, Libby placed her right hand over her heart as she thanked them all for their years of support, belief, and dedication. Around the room, many people's eyes were moist and they held their fingers to their lips. Libby's hand to her heart reflected her appreciation.

Fingers placed over the mouth indicate that they're keeping something from coming out.

Gesturing to illustrate what you're saying

When you describe an object, you frequently use gestures to illustrate what the object is like. Your listener finds it easier to understand what you're saying when you let your body create a picture of the object rather than relying on words alone. If you're describing a round object, like a ball, for example, you may hold your hands in front of yourself with your fingers arched upward and your thumbs pointing down. Describing a square building you may draw vertical and horizontal lines with a flat hand, cutting through the space like a knife. If you're telling someone about a turbulent ride on a boat or plane, your arms and hands may beat up and down in rhythmic fashion. Describing a large object may entail holding your arms out wide. If you're illustrating a small point you may hold your fingers close together. The point is that gesturing is a useful means of conveying visual information.

Because some people take in information more effectively by seeing what's being described, illustrating your message through gestures helps create a clear picture for them. To help someone who can't see, to experience what you're describing, hold her hands in the appropriate position.

As Lotsie was describing her climb up Mount Kilimanjaro she acted out those moments when the air felt so thin that she was hardly able to breathe and when she struggled to put one foot in front of the other. She mimed leaning on her walking stick, bending over with the weight of her equipment, gasping for air, and pausing between shuffled steps as she put one foot in front of the other. Her gestures painted the combined picture of a woman who was both fit and exhausted.

Physically supporting the spoken word

Gesturing can add emphasis to your voice, clarify your meaning, and give impact to your message. Whether your point requires a gentle approach, or a firm telling off, your body's instinct is to reflect and move in harmony with the emotion.

In addition to reinforcing your message, hand signals especially reflect your desire for your message to be taken seriously. Watch a well-schooled politician standing at the podium. See how the hands move in a precise, controlled manner. No wasted gestures, just those specific ones that paint a clear picture and accurately convey the message.

Experienced lawyers, celebrities, and anyone in the public arena are also adept at emphasising their messages through considered movements and gestures. By carefully timing, focusing, and controlling their actions, moving in synchronicity with their spoken words, and responding appropriately to the atmosphere in their environment, they court and woo the people they want, and dismiss others with aplomb.

When you're giving bad news and want to soften the blow, adapt your body language to reflect empathy. Move close to the person you're comforting and tilt your body towards hers. You may even touch her on the hand or arm, or place your arm around her shoulder.

When you're making a formal presentation, use gestures to help your audience remember the points you're making.

During the introduction to your presentation, as you establish the points to be covered, list them separately on your fingers. You may hold them up in front of you, or touch your fingers individually on one hand with a finger from your other hand as you say the point. (Note: Most British and American people begin counting with their index finger. Many Europeans begin counting with their thumb.) When talking about point 1 in your presentation, point the first finger, or gesture to it; when you reach point two, point or gesture to your second finger, and so on.

Revealing thoughts, attitudes, and beliefs

You don't have to tell people how you're feeling for them to know. Look at Rodin's sculpture of *The Thinker*. There can be no doubt about that person's state of mind: thoughtful, serious, and contemplative. Equally so, a child throwing a tantrum with stomping feet, clenched fists, and a screwed up face is letting you know that she's not happy.

Think of your body as if it were a movie screen. The information to be projected is inside you and your body is the vehicle onto which the information is displayed. Whether you're anxious, excited, happy, or sad, your body shows the world what's going on inside. Here are some examples:

- ✔ People who feel threatened or unsure of themselves touch themselves as a means of self-comfort or self-restraint. Gestures, such as rubbing their foreheads, crossing their arms, and holding or rubbing their fingers in front of their mouths, provide comfort and protection (see Figure 1-1).

- ✔ People who perform specific gestures reserved for religious rituals reveal their beliefs and values. Upon entering a Catholic church, the congregation dip their fingers into holy water and cross themselves. Before entering the home of many Jewish people, you may touch the mezuzah by the front door. Muslims bow in prayer facing east. By performing these gestures, people are demonstrating their respect for the culture, its traditions, and values.

- ✔ People in a state of elation often breathe in deeply and gesture outwards with expanded arms. Pictures of winning sportspeople frequently show them in the open position with their arms extended, their heads thrown back, and their mouths and eyes opened in ecstasy.

- ✔ Footballers who miss the penalty kick and city traders who get their numbers wrong often walk dejectedly with their heads down, and their hands clasped behind their necks. The hand position is a comforting gesture and the head facing downwards shows that the individual's upset.

Figure 1-1: These two men are telling us they're disagreeing about something.

✔ People in despair, or feeling down and depressed, reveal their thoughts and attitudes by the slouch in their step, their drooping heads, and their downward cast eyes. Positive people, on the other hand, reveal their thoughts and attitudes with an upright stance, a bounce in their step, and eyes that appear lively and engaged.

✔ Not every bent head signals depression. Sometimes it just means that you're reflecting, thinking, or absorbing information. If you're demonstrating the behaviour of someone who's thinking hard, your head most likely rests in your hand or on your fingertips, like Rodin's *The Thinker*.

At Peter and Louise's wedding anniversary celebrations, Peter stood up to toast his wife and children. As he raised his glass to the family members, his feelings for them were clear. By the way he slightly leaned forward toward his son, Sebastian, you were able to sense the great warmth and tenderness he held for him. As he turned to his daughter Olivia, to express his amazement at her joyous spirit, he slightly lifted his head and tossed it back. When he turned to gaze at his wife Louise, his eyes softened and a gentle smile played at the sides of his mouth. He stood upright, held his arm forward, and raised his glass high.

Holding your hands over or near your heart, as shown in Figure 1-2, is an expression of how much something means to you.

Figure 1-2: The hands over the heart, the tilted head, and the open smile indicate appreciation.

Key Types of Gestures

Humans are blessed with the ability to create a wide variety of gestures and expressions from the top of the head to the tips of the toes. Gestures can show intention, such as leaning forward just before rising out of a chair; as well as showing no intention, such as crossing arms and legs. Some gestures belong to you, because you've become so identifiable by them. Some gestures are displacement gestures: you do them for no reason other than to displace some energy. Some gestures are specific to local customs, and some are universal gestures that everyone does.

Unintentional gestures

Unintentional gestures are behaviours that inhibit your ability to act. They're like the fright part in the 'fright or flight' syndrome.

The unintentional gestures imply that you have no intention of moving from where you are. They hold you back, won't let you go, and your body says that you're not budging. And no amount of outside influence to get you to move is going to succeed.

Examples of unintentional gestures are

- ✔ Folded arms
- ✔ Lips pressed together
- ✔ A hand or finger in front of the mouth
- ✔ Crossed legs

These actions all keep you in place. You can't walk when your legs are crossed. You can't speak with your hand in front of your mouth. Crossed arms say that you're holding back.

Standing or sitting with your legs crossed is no position to take if you want to get out of town quickly. The scissor stance is a prime example of a gesture that keeps you in your place. One leg is crossed over the other, rendering you immobile (see Figure 1-3). When someone adopts this position you know she's staying put.

Because the scissor stance contains no sign of impatience, the gesture can come across as submissive. The person has no forward movement in her body as in the body of a person about to take action. The person who acts is usually considered to be dominant. Therefore, the person who stays put is usually considered to be submissive.

Figure 1-3: The finger over the mouth and the scissored legs indicate she's holding back.

Signature gestures: Gestures that define who you are

A signature gesture is one that you become known by, a common gesture that you perform in a particular way. The person who twirls her curls around her finger, or the one who sucks her thumb, or the one who pats her eyebrows. These gestures give us clues into the person's personality.

Signature gestures set you apart from all others. Think Napoleon Bonaparte and his mighty stance (see Figure 1-4) – on the canvas, not the battlefield. Standing with his hand tucked into his waistcoat, he looks the picture of pride and authority. Who knows if he ever really stood in that position. The artist created the image and we believe the artist.

Figure 1-4: The Bonaparte pose conveys stature and authority.

One of Diana, Princess of Wales's most vividly remembered signature gesture's was the head lowered, eyes looking upward, now known as the Shy Di look (see Figure 1-5).

Sophie is a delightful woman in her early twenties. Pretty, vivacious, and polite, Sophie's signature gesture is thumb-sucking. I first noticed this gesture when she spent several days at our home. Curled up on the couch, Sophie slipped her right thumb into her mouth, lightly rubbing her nose with her index finger. Claire, a woman in her forties, also sucks her thumb. Her variation on this gesture is a small piece of soft fabric that she rubs in the palm of her cupped hand.

Toby, my personal assistant, is a quiet, thoughtful, focused man. I'm highly energetic with a mind that skips and leaps from one project to the next. Frequently, I ask Toby to do one task, only to interrupt his concentration by asking him to do something else, often unrelated. When Toby pats his eyebrows with the tips of his fingers I know that the time's come for me to back off and let him get on with what he has to do.

Figure 1-5: A downward tilted head and upcast eyes looks vulnerable and pleading.

Some examples of signature gestures can be seen in a person's

- ✓ Posture
- ✓ Smile
- ✓ Hand clap
- ✓ Pointing finger
- ✓ Clothes tugging

Some sportspeople perform specific actions as an anchor to get them grounded and focus their energy. Before serving, the tennis player Rafael Nadal, tugs at the back of his shorts. This gesture is so closely associated with this gifted sportsman that other players have been known to mock him on the courts and in the dressing rooms by performing it in front of him.

By recognising signature gestures you can tell what kind of person you're dealing with. Certain gestures, like clapping the hands together once, show a mind that's organised. The hair twirling gesture indicates that the person may be a day dreamer. When you successfully read the signs you can figure out how best to manage the person.

If you want to be easily identified and remembered you can create your own signature gesture. Victoria Beckham's sexily defiant pout has become her signature gesture, as has Hugh Grant's foppish head toss.

Fake gestures: Pulling the wool

Fake gestures are designed to camouflage, conceal, and fool. They deliberately point you in one direction to make you believe something that isn't so. Fake gestures pretend to be something when they're actually something else.

You're able to tell a fake gesture from a real one because some of the real gesture's parts are missing.

Some gestures that are commonly faked are

- ✔ Smiling
- ✔ Frowning
- ✔ Sighing
- ✔ Crying
- ✔ Holding your body as if in pain

Anna is a highly motivated recently qualified lawyer in a large London firm. She knows that, in part, her success depends on her ability to get on well with clients and colleagues. One day her supervising partner invited her to attend a client meeting and to put together the remaining briefs that a previous trainee had begun and hadn't had time to finish. Anna, already overloaded with work, stayed at the office until well past midnight. In spite of little sleep and over an hour's commute that morning, she arrived, shortly before the meeting's 8 a.m. start looking smart. At one point during the session the client remarked that some information seemed to be missing. The partner shot Anna a glance of annoyance before covering up his feelings with the hearty remark, 'Well, she's new on the job. We'll let her get away with it just this once.' To cover her fury and shame, Anna put on what she calls her 'smiley face', a big toothy grin, and offered to find the missing materials. Anna's teeth were clenched, and her eyes didn't crinkle (a sign of a sincere smile). She was tired, hurt, and humiliated and anyone paying attention would have seen she was giving a fake grin.

Look for all the signs. Fake gestures are meant to deceive.

Micro gestures: A little gesture means a lot

Teeny weeny, so small that they sometimes take highly specialised equipment to see them, micro gestures are flashes of emotion that flicker across your face faster than a hummingbird, revealing feelings that you may prefer to keep to yourself. These gestures aren't ones that you purposely choose. Micro gestures give a brief hint of what's going on inside. You choose to smile, wave, and rise from a chair. You don't choose to have a micro gesture flicker across your face. No one is immune to them.

A list of the more common micro gestures include

- ✔ Movement around the mouth
- ✔ Tension at the eyes
- ✔ Flaring of the nose

Mark and Liz met at a party. They were immediately attracted to one another. They stood easily in the other's intimate space. Their facial gestures were controlled, but the occasional flicker around Liz's eyes and hint of a smile around Mark's mouth gave the impression that a frisson existed between the two. Friends and family members recognised the signs and frequently ask about the relationship between Liz and Mark.

Displacement gestures

When you're feeling conflicting emotions, you may engage in gestures that have no relation to your immediate goals. These behaviours are mostly self-directed and serve to release excess energy and gain a feeling of comfort, even if only temporary. Drumming fingers, flicking feet, going for a glass of water when you're not even thirsty – these are the behaviours of someone who's looking to burn some pent up energy, or at least, refocus it. Called displacement activities, they're a conduit for excess energy that's looking for a place to go.

Some examples of displacement gestures are

- ✔ Fiddling with objects
- ✔ Tugging at your earlobe
- ✔ Straightening your clothes
- ✔ Stroking your chin
- ✔ Running your fingers through your hair
- ✔ Eating
- ✔ Smoking

Some smokers light up a cigarette, take a puff or two, and then put it out or leave it in the ashtray barely smoked. These people may not actually want the cigarette, but need a gesture to take their mind off something else.

I knew the time had come to stop smoking when I had three cigarettes on the go in a four-room apartment. I was working in New York, living on my own, making barely enough to pay my monthly bills, and wondering what I was doing with my life. I was frustrated and feeling anxious. One morning, while I was in the kitchen making coffee, I lit up a cigarette. When the phone rang, I answered it in the living room, leaving the cigarette burning in the kitchen. While speaking on the phone to my soon-to-be ex-husband I lit another cigarette which, after a drag or two, I stubbed out in the ashtray on my desk. I went to the bathroom to get ready for work. Here, too, I lit a cigarette, which I occasionally puffed on as I applied my make-up. In the course of less than 10 minutes I had lit three cigarettes, none of which I was interested in smoking.

Rather than stating their feelings verbally, people demonstrating displacement activities are letting their gestures reveal their emotion.

Prince Charles is noted for fiddling with his cufflinks. He crosses his arm over his body and touches his cufflinks in a protective and reassuring gesture. The Prince is displacing his anxiety by making contact with his cufflinks. On honeymoon with Diana, the late Princess of Wales, Charles is purported to have worn cufflinks given to him by his current wife, the Duchess of Cornwall. No wonder that his young bride was upset when she discovered this wedding gift of gold cufflinks with entwined Cs. Especially when she saw him fondling them.

Words convey information. Gestures reveal attitude. If someone's feeling anxious she may fiddle with her keys, twist the ring on her finger, or pull at her clothes to compensate for her anxiety.

If you see someone under pressure and being scrutinised, look to see what her hands are doing. If she's gently rubbing her stomach, you may assume that she's feeling the pressure and is calming and comforting himself, the way you comfort a baby or sick child.

Universal gestures

Universal gestures, such as blushing, smiling, and the wide-eyed expression of fear, mean the same thing across world cultures. These gestures stem from human biological make-up, which is why you can recognise them spanning the globe.

Smiling

From the sands of Iraq to the shores of Malibu, humans are born with the ability to smile. From the earliest days in an infant's life, her facial muscles can form the upward turn of the lips and the crinkling around the outer edges of the eyes to create a recognisable smile.

Sure, each person may have her own unique way of smiling. The point remains that anyone with working facial muscles who's conveying a positive message lifts her lips in pleasure.

When you see the sides of the lips turned up and the eyes crinkling at their outer edges, count on that smile being genuine in showing pleasure.

The Japanese smile in embarrassment as well as pleasure. Young women giggle behind their hands. Don't expect the Japanese to respond to your humour with a raucous, belly laugh.

Blushing

If you blush, your embarrassment's showing. The blood flows to your chest and cheeks, and you want to drop down and hide. Go to Thailand, go to Alabama, or any country: You see this gesture everywhere when embarrassment takes over.

To control the blushing take several slow, deep breaths from your diaphragm to steady your nerves and control the blood flow.

My Aunt MarNell lives in Dallas, Texas and is the perfect combination of cowgirl and southern belle. When Dad, MarNell's only sibling and adored brother, raised his glass in special toast to her, her cheeks flushed like a young girl's.

Crying

Crying is a universal sign of sadness. One of an infant's first actions is to let out a walloping great cry when she first enters this world, having been torn for the comfort and safety of her mother's womb. No one had to teach her, she was born knowing how.

If you feel tears well up in your eyes and you want to stop them from flowing down your face, fix your gaze at that point where the ceiling and wall meet.

Shrugging

Shrugging is a gesture that people use when they need to protect themselves in some way. The full shrug is when your head dips into your rising shoulders, the sides of your mouth turn down, your palms turn upwards, and you raise your eyebrows.

The shrug can indicate

- Indifference
- Disdain
- Unknowing
- Embarrassment

To know which attitude is being expressed, you have to look to see what the other body parts are doing.

I was invited to speak at an event for Women in Technology. I made the mistake of sitting at the panel table before making my presentation, rather than joining them afterwards. When the host introduced me her comments were so glowing that I felt embarrassed. I had set myself up for all to see and, rather than squaring my shoulders and lifting my head with pride, I dropped my head and lifted my shoulders in a humble shrug, as if seeking protection. What saved me from looking like a complete idiot was the sparkle in my eye and the bounce in my step when I took to the floor.

Getting the Most Out of Body Language

Successful people know how to use their bodies for greatest effect. They stand tall, with their chests opened like a well loved book, smiles on their faces, and when they move, they move with purpose. Their moderate and carefully chosen gestures reflect their sense of what they want to project and how they want to be perceived.

Successful people also know where to position themselves in relation to other people. They know that if they stand too close they can be perceived as overwhelming or threatening. They know that if they stand too far away they can be perceived as distant. They know how to anticipate movements – theirs and another's – to avoid (or not) bumping into someone else, depending on their motives, and their relationship with the other person. They know that the gestures they use and how they use them have infinitely more of an impact than the words they say.

The people who demonstrate respect for others, who think before acting, and who develop the necessary skills to create their desired outcomes, are the ones who feel good about themselves. You can tell by the way they move. Their gestures and actions have purpose and meaning.

If you want to succeed in your career or relationship, using effective body language is part of your foundation. Once you're aware of the impact – of what works and what doesn't – you can move and gesture with confidence, knowing that you and your message are perceived the way you want them to be.

Becoming spatially aware

Understanding how to position themselves in relation to other people is a skill that some people just don't seem to have. Either they're so up close and personal that you can smell their morning coffee breath, or they stand just that bit away that makes them appear uninterested, unengaged, or slightly removed. Others, however, know just how to get it right. They understand and respect the different territories and parameters that people have around themselves, and being with them is comfortable.

You have a personal, individual space bubble that you stand, sit, and move around in, and it expands and contracts depending on circumstances. Although you may have grown up in the country and have need for a lot of space around you, people who grew up in cities need less.

The study of *proxemics*, how people use and relate to the space around them to communicate, was pioneered by Edward T Hall, an American anthropologist in the 1960s. His findings revealed the different amounts of personal space that people feel they need depending on their social situation. Robert Sommer, an American psychologist, coined the term 'personal space' in 1969. He defined it as the 'comfortable separation zone' people like to have around them.

Chapter 10 takes a look at how circumstances determine at what distance you're most comfortable, and how best to position yourself in relation to another person, whether standing, sitting, or lying down.

Anticipating movements

Movement can be equated to dance. It's more than just the gestures themselves, it's about the timing of them as well. Anticipating an action and registering that it's about to happen before it does, gives you information that others may not grasp.

The American anthropologist, Ray Birdwhistell, pioneered kinesics, the study of body movement and verbal communication. Replaying, in slow motion, films of people in conversation Birdwhistell was able to analyse people's actions, gestures, and behaviours.

Consider these examples:

- ✔ Spotting the subtle gestures a person makes in preparation for rising from a seated position previews what's about to happen.

- ✔ Recognising when a person's about to strike out in anger gives you enough time to protect yourself and others.

- ✔ Feeling your dancing partner shift his weight indicates that a change in movement is about to occur.

Anticipating a movement can save your life. It can keep you from harm. It may also bring you great happiness, like a lover's first kiss which, had you missed the movement, you may have lost. By anticipating gestures, you gain the upper hand in knowing how to respond before the action is completed.

Creating rapport through reflecting gestures

When you talk about establishing rapport you're talking about accepting and connecting with other people and treating one another with respect. Rapport assures that your communications are effective and lead to results that satisfy both parties' needs.

You have many ways of creating rapport, through touch, word choice, and eye contact. Another way is to reflect another person's movements. By mirroring and matching the other person's gestures and behaviours you're demonstrating that you know what it feels, sounds, and looks like to be in her shoes. If connecting with others and behaving respectfully is important to you, mirroring and matching their behaviour helps you achieve that goal.

A fine line exists between reflecting another person's gestures and mimicking her. People who are being mimicked quickly figure out what you're doing and recognise your insincerity.

Becoming who you want to be

How you present yourself, how you move and gesture, how you stand, sit, and walk all play their part in creating the image you present and in determining people's perceptions. By adopting a cluster of postures, positions, and gestures known for the attitudes they effect, you can create any attitude and make it your own. Positive body language looks and feels strong, engaged, and vibrant. Negative body language communicates weaknesses, dullness, and a disconnectedness. Sometimes you want to project one image over another. Whatever image you want to project – moving your head, face, torso, and limbs with confidence, control, and commitment, or creating desired effects with the flick of your wrist or a furrow of your brow – being perceived and responded to in the way you want helps you to achieve your desired results.

Actors know the technique of creating a character from both within and without. Working from the outside in, actors consider how their character sounds, moves, and gestures. They ask themselves:

- ✔ How would the character walk, sit, and stand? Would the character move like a gazelle, lumber along like a sleepy bear, or stagger in a zigzag pattern like someone who's had one drink too many? Is the posture upright and erect, or slouched and limp?

- ✔ What gestures would be required for conveying a particular mood or emotion? Slow, deliberate, and carefully timed gestures create a different impression from those that are quick, spontaneous, and unfocused.

By adopting the appropriate behaviours, the actor creates an attitude, emotion, or feeling that the audience recognises and understands. It's the same for the lay person. By acting in a particular manner you can create an image and become that character. As Cary Grant said, 'I pretended to be someone I wanted to be until I finally became that person.'

The behaviour you adopt and the gestures that you make leave an impression. How you're perceived – dumb or sultry, champion of the people, or chairman of the board – is up to you. The key is to adopt/exhibit/display the right gestures. To do that, keep these points in mind:

- ✔ **Make sure that your gestures reinforce the impression you want to make:** For example, the higher up the command chain, the more contained the gesture (which is why you never see the chief executive run down the hall).

- ✔ **You can modify your gestures to suit the situation:** When Toby, my PA and I, are working in the office and no one else is around, our body language is loose and relaxed. When a client or another colleague arrives, the body language changes. We both become more formal, the degree of formality depending on the other person.

Decide what attitude you want to project. Model the gestures of a person who you think successfully emulates that image.

I recently experienced my first tax audit, which had me in a bit of a state. Tom, my bookkeeper, and my accountant Rashmi, tell me how much and where to sign and I do it. I trust them and Tom's been teaching me about the finances. Tom arrived at the office, wearing a suit and tie, for the meeting with the VAT lady. Our office is normally quite informal and Tom's change of clothes told me that we were to leave out the jokes. Although I was dressed informally I adjusted my behaviour to mirror Tom's, which was thoughtful, serious, and open. We wanted to create the impression that not only does the business have a strong creative base, but also that its financial backbone is firmly in place.

Reading the signs and responding appropriately

Being able to read other's signals is a stepping stone to effective communication. By observing how people move and gesture, you get a glimpse into their emotions. You can tell, for example, the intensity of someone's feelings by the way she stands. You can see what kind of mood a person's in by the speed of her gestures. By having an insight into someone's feelings you're forewarned and forearmed for whatever may happen next.

Say that you're at a party with a friend. You notice her sitting dejectedly by herself. Seeing her in this position, with her head hanging down and her arms wrapped around her body, you know that she needs a little tender loving care. You gently put your hand on her arm and she begins to feel a bit better.

Later at the party you observe that some of the younger guests – who have had more than their fair share of drink – are beginning to go from jovial to rowdy. You notice the lads pushing and shoving one another, which is your sign to leave.

By reading body language effectively, you can tell when you can stay and when to go.

Edith unexpectedly popped around to have a chat with her neighbours, Tim and Sarah, who were in the middle of a busy morning and had little time to stop for a gossip. Although Tim smiled warmly at Edith, he stood by the entrance without inviting her in. His arms were crossed over his chest, his legs were held closely together, and rhythmically he rocked backwards and forwards on his toes. Edith sensed from Tim's closed position that now was not a convenient time for them to speak, and she quickly left.

Appreciating Cultural Differences

How much more exciting, interesting, and stimulating it is to live in a world with difference and diversity, rather than one in which everything's the same. Even though you appreciate the differences between cultures and nationalities, you may sometimes find yourself confused, scared, or even repelled by displays of body language that are very different from what you're used to.

Because people in one culture act differently than people in another doesn't suggest that one is right and the other is wrong. When it comes to cultural differences, the operative verbs are 'to respect' and 'to value'. Valuing behaviours that vary so much from those that you grew up with, and were taught to believe in, can be hard. To create respectful, positive relationships between different cultures and nationalities, you need to expand the way you think and work, from an attitude of respect. That doesn't mean having to agree with all the behaviours you see in your travels. Instead, accept that differences do exist, and then decide how best to respond.

Chapter 12 looks at different cultures and how behaviour and body language impact upon communication between nations.

Different nationalities and cultures use their bodies differently. An acceptable gesture in one country may land you in jail in another. Before visiting or moving to another country, do your homework and find out what's suitable and what's not. Before making a gesture, think whether it's appropriate and acceptable before doing so.

Chapter 2

Looking Closer at Non-verbal Gestures

. . . .

In This Chapter

▶ Looking into the origins of body language

▶ Conveying information through body language

▶ Considering gestures – what you can discover from others

. . . .

*W*hether you like to think of yourself as an animal or not, the truth is, you are. And like all animals, the way you gesture, move, and position your body tells an observer a lot more about you than the words you say.

Throughout the animal kingdom, body language is a constant and reliable form of communication. Whether on two, four, or more legs, homo sapiens and the rest of the animal kingdom are constantly sizing one another up as they prepare for a friendly, or unfriendly, encounter. Because of the structure and programming of the human body, it's capable of sending a myriad silent messages, whereas most animals are limited in the number of signals they can convey.

In this chapter, I revisit our ancient ancestors to see where body language began and how it evolved. You discover that the way you use your body conveys how you're feeling, what you're thinking, and your general state of being. You find out how body language reveals the feelings and attitudes you may prefer to leave unsaid, as well as how it supports your spoken message.

The History of Body Language

For over 100 years psychologists, anthropologists, and even zoologists have been studying non-verbal behaviour throughout the animal kingdom to understand its implications and explore its possible applications in the broader field of human communication. These experts recognise that applying that knowledge of non-verbal behaviour in practical settings allows people to communicate more successfully than if they rely purely on the spoken word.

Research into primate behaviour concludes that non-verbal behaviour, including gestures and facial expressions, is a reliable source for conveying messages.

Aping our ancestors

Charles Darwin concluded that humans' ability to express emotions, feelings, and attitudes through posture and gesture, stems from prehistoric apes that most resemble today's chimpanzees. Like humans, chimpanzees are social animals that live in groups. As with humans, chimpanzees' needs are based around successful communication and cooperation in order to survive. As chimpanzees have yet to develop the ability to speak, they primarily rely on non-vocal means such as stance, facial expressions, and touching gestures, to show who's in charge and where there's danger.

Darwin published his findings in *The Expression of the Emotions in Man and Animals* in 1872. Regarded as the most influential pre-20th century work on the subject of body language, this academic study continues to serve as the foundation for modern investigations into facial expressions and non-verbal behaviour. Close to 140 years after its original publication, Darwin's findings about posture, gesture, and expression are consistently validated by experts in the field.

Gestures first, language second

Further research into the foundations of communication suggests that spoken language evolved from gesture. In evolutionary terms, speech is a relatively new means of communication, having only been a part of humans' communication process for somewhere between 500,000 and 2 million years.

According to Frans de Waal of the Yerkes National Primate Research Center in Atlanta, Georgia, gestures appeared first in human development, followed by speech. Babies quickly discover which gestures to use, and how to use them to get what they want.

Studying the behaviour patterns of apes and monkeys, de Waal concludes that gestures used as specific signals are a more recent addition to the communication chain, coming after vocalisations and facial expressions. Apes (which are genetically closer to humans than monkeys are) use specific gestures but monkeys don't.

Although humans' ability to communicate effectively has evolved with the development of speech, body language continues to be the most reliable source for conveying attitude, feelings, and emotions.

The Nuts and Bolts of Body Language

The primary purpose of the spoken word is to convey information, facts, and data whereas body language is designed to relay attitudes, feelings, thoughts, and emotions. You may argue that words also relay attitudes, feelings, thoughts, and emotions, and you'd be right. Sometimes. Think back to those occasions when you said words like, 'I'm fine; there's no problem; I think you're great; I couldn't be happier' when you really meant, 'I'm annoyed; there's a huge problem; I think you're hideous; I couldn't be more miserable.' If the person you were speaking to was a careful observer he would have noticed that while your words were giving one message, the way you delivered them signalled a conflicting meaning.

The meaning of a gesture depends on the context in which it's used, as well as on what other signals are being sent out at the same time.

Context clues: Studying gestures in chimps and bonobos

Studying humans' closest primate relatives – chimpanzees and the black-faced bonobo chimpanzees – research conducted by Amy Pollick and Frans de Waal concluded that the meaning of a gesture depends on the context in which it's made, as well as other gestures that are occurring at the same time. Observing a captive test group of chimps and bonobos, the researchers identified 31 gestures – defined as any movement of the forearm, hand, wrist, or fingers, used solely for the purpose of communication. In addition, they identified 18 facial or vocal signals and recorded them in the context in which they were made. The facial and vocal signals had practically the same meaning in the two species. The gestures had different meanings.

The common signal for fear in chimps is a 'bared-tooth scream'. The 'up and out' gesture of reaching with the palm facing upward has different meanings. Depending on the context, it can be interpreted as begging for food or money as street beggars do, or begging for a friend's support. The open-handed gesture can frequently be seen after a fight where reconciliation is sought. This versatility demonstrates the necessity for context to be taken into consideration before interpreting the meaning of a gesture.

Kinesics: The categories of gesture

The American anthropologist Ray Birdwhistell was a pioneer in the study of non-verbal behaviour. He labelled this form of communication 'kinesics' as it relates to movement of individual body parts, or the body as a whole. Building on Birdwhistell's work, Professor Paul Ekman and his colleague Wallace V Friesen classified kinesics into five categories: emblems, illustrators, affective displays, regulators, and adapters.

Kinesics convey specific meanings that are open to cultural interpretation. The movements can be misinterpreted when communicating across cultures as most of them are carried out with little if any awareness. In today's global environment, awareness of the meanings of different kinesic movements is important in order to avoid sending the wrong message.

Emblems

Emblems are non-verbal signals with a verbal equivalent. Emblems are easily identified because they're frequently used in specific contexts. The person receiving the gesture immediately understands what it means.

Examples of emblems include:

- ✔ **The V-shaped sign.** Winston Churchill made the victory sign popular. The palm of the hand faces forwards with the middle and forefingers held erect.

- ✔ **The raised arm and tightly closed fist.** Generally the fist is used as an expression of solidarity or defiance. In 1990 Nelson Mandela walked free of prison holding this position. Amongst black rights activists in the United States the raised fist is known as the black power salute.

- ✔ **The Finger.** Americans hold the middle finger of the hand in an upright position, with the back of the hand facing out. In Britian it's more common to hold up your index and middle fingers with the back of your hand facing out. Both gestures mean the same thing and the meaning's quite rude.

- ✔ **The Sign of the Cuckold.** Your index and little fingers are extended pointing forward with your palm facing down, making 'horns'. Your thumb crosses over your two middle fingers. You're telling an Italian that his partner's been unfaithful. In Texas, this gesture is the sign for fans of the University of Texas Longhorns football team and has nothing to do with infidelity.

Because of different interpretations of the same gesture between cultures, the correct reading is dependent on the context in which the signal occurs.

Illustrators

Illustrators create a visual image and support the spoken message. They tend to be subconscious movements occurring more regularly than emblematic kinesic movements.

Example: Holding your hands apart to indicate size.

The usage and the amount of illustrators used differ from culture to culture. In general, Latinos use illustrators more than their Anglo-Saxon counterparts, who make more use of illustrators than many Asian cultures. In some Asian cultures, extensive use of illustrators is often interpreted as a lack of intelligence. In Latin cultures, the absence of illustrators indicates a lack of interest.

Affective displays

Affective displays tend to be movements, usually facial gestures, displaying specific emotions. They're less conscious than illustrators and occur less frequently. Although they convey universal emotions and can be understood fairly easily, the degree and frequency with which they occur is determined by cultural mores.

Example: Expressions of love, frustration, or anger.

A lack of affective displays doesn't indicate a lack of emotion. Cultural considerations determine what is considered to be acceptable behaviour. A person from Japan expressing anger shows significantly fewer affective display movements than his Italian counterpart. This doesn't suggest, however, that the Japanese person is feeling any less annoyed. The Japanese are taught to hold in their emotions whereas Italians are encouraged to express them fully.

Regulators

Regulators – body movements that control, adjust, and sustain the flow of a conversation – are frequently relied on to feedback how much of the message the listener has understood.

Example: Head nodding and eye movements.

Because of cultural differences in the use of regulators, the way in which people respond to the flow of information can be confusing. A misinterpreted regulatory signal in international politics and business can lead to serious problems.

Adaptors

Adaptors include changes in posture and other movements, made with little awareness. These body adjustments are to perform a specific function, or to make the person more comfortable. Because they occur with such a low level of awareness, they're considered to be the keys to understanding what someone really thinks. Adaptors principally comprise body-focussed movements, such as rubbing, touching, scratching, and so on.

Example: Shifting body and/or feet position when seated.

The significance given to adaptors may be overstated as well as oversimplified. Many adaptor movements, such as shifting position while seated, may be simply a way of resolving a specific physical situation, such as being uncomfortable, rather than revealing emotions and attitudes.

Inborn responses

A newborn baby latches onto its mother's breast and begins to suckle. A child born blind and deaf smiles, frowns, and cries. These reactions aren't taught. Inborn responses to specific stimuli such as these require no practice or knowledge and are performed unconsciously, unprompted, and without self-analysis.

Some movements are so familiar that you take them completely for granted. Asked how to do them and you wouldn't have a clue. Take for example, interlocking fingers. Every person has a dominant thumb, which consistently rests on top of the other when you interlock your fingers. If you were asked which of your thumbs rests on top you probably wouldn't know and would have to have a look to find out. This doesn't mean that you can't reverse the position and put the other thumb on top. Do it and see what happens. Feels strange, awkward, and not quite right, doesn't it?

The study of animal behaviour, especially as it occurs in a natural environment, was pioneered by Irenaus Eibl-Eibesfeldt, an Austrian scientist and head of the Max Planck Institute for Behavioural Physiology in Germany. His interest in humans as 'signal carriers' significantly contributed to the field of Human Ethology, including the study of inborn actions.

The way an inborn action works is like this. Think of your brain as being programmed like a computer. It's encoded to connect precise reactions with particular stimuli involving inputs and outputs. The stimuli, or input, triggers a reaction, or output. The process is straightforward and simple, requiring no prior experience or learned behaviour.

An example of inborn behaviour is the rapid raising and lowering of the eyebrows as a sign of greeting, a gesture that can be seen around the world. Stamping feet in anger and baring teeth when enraged also seem to be inborn behaviours. It seems that no matter how far humans evolve from their prehistoric relatives, the basic urges and actions remain the same.

Learned gestures

The English zoologist, human behavioural scientist, and author, Desmond Morris, believes that human beings have an abundant variety of actions that, in addition to being genetically inherited, are learned behaviours. Some of these behaviours are discovered, others are absorbed, some are taught, and still others are acquired in a combination of ways.

Discovering actions for yourself

Most people around the world are born with similar hands, arms, and legs, and move and gesture with them in pretty much the same way. An African warrior, a London banker, and a Minnesota farmer with their similar arms, all discover, at some point in their lives, how to fold them across their chests. No one taught them how to take that pose. During the growing up process, as they became familiar with their bodies, they unconsciously discovered they were able to do this. Most of the time you don't even know how you perform the gesture. When you cross your arms over your chest, which one's on top? See what I mean?

Absorbed actions

Observe a group of teenage girls, watch the guys in the boardroom, or the celebrities on the red carpet and you notice that within each grouping a similar pattern of behaviour exists. Humans are imitative characters, easily influenced by the actions of others, especially if the others are considered to be of a higher status. The higher the status, the more they're copied. Without being aware of it, the people within the individual groups reflect one another's actions, gestures, postures, and expressions.

You absorb most from those you admire.

Trained actions

Some actions have to be learned. For example, say you want to wink. You give it a go and it doesn't quite work. You give it another go. This time it's a little better, still with plenty of room for improvement. Desperate to be an adept winker, you deliberately and doggedly practise until you manage it. You learn how to wink.

Most of you aren't going to join the circus, where somersaulting and walking on your hands is required, but at some time in your lives you shake hands with other people. Having an adept teacher helps. Watch a parent teaching his child how to shake hands properly and you see a trained action being taught.

Refined actions

Several categories of actions influence the many behaviours you perform in your adult life. Some, like crying, are inborn. As an infant you cried uncontrollably. As a toddler you wept and shouted. As an adult you can still let your emotions all hang out or suppress your sobs, depending on local cultural influences.

Consider the way you cross your legs. As a child you discover that sitting with your legs crossed is a comfortable position. You do it without thinking. Then society intervenes. As you mature, the way you cross your legs emulates other members of your sex, nationality, age group, and social class. And you don't even notice it's happening.

At times, when you're mixing with people you don't know too well, you may feel uncomfortable, without knowing why. The reason is because the others are moving, acting, and gesticulating in a manner different to yours. Even though the differences may be subtle, they're detectable.

A Final Word on Non-verbal Gestures

Charlie Chaplin, Gloria Swanson, and all the other great actors of the silent screen knew how to use their bodies, gestures, and facial expressions to convey messages to their audiences. With the advent of the talkies, the only actors who survived were those who were able to communicate successfully by combining their vocal and physical skills. Many a pretty face fell onto the cutting room floor for want of a decent voice.

Dancers, mimes, and people with speech impairments face a similar challenge of conveying emotion without relying on the spoken word. They rely solely on position, movement, and expression to reveal their inner thoughts, feelings, and attitudes.

You don't have to be a professional performer for your body to reveal, both consciously and subconsciously, your emotions, attitudes, and beliefs. Nor do you have to be a mind-reader to understand the people you interact with. You simply need to be aware of and understand gestures – those you make and those you see. Some are subtle, some are obvious. Some seek to share; others seek to hide. But all are revealing – if you know what to look for.

The remaining parts of this book look at the various types of signals and gestures (researchers have observed and documented almost one million of them!) that the body sends and offer advice on how you can use the power of body language to improve your own communications.

Part II
Starting at the Top

The 5th Wave   By Rich Tennant

"They've been that way for over 10 minutes. Larry's either having a staring contest with the customer, or he's afraid to ask for the sale again."

In this part . . .

1 head straight to the top and explore how you can read eyes and facial expressions. They say the eyes are the windows to the soul, and you'd better believe it. The chapters in the part help you discover how the tilt of your head and the size of your pupils reveal more than words can say.

Chapter 3

Heading to the Heart of the Matter

· ·

In This Chapter

▶ Using your head to display power

▶ Nodding your head in agreement

▶ Tilting your head to indicate interest

▶ Discerning the meaning of other head movements

· ·

*W*hether you hold your head high, cant it in contrition, or drop it in despair, the way you position your head reveals what you think of the person, place, or thing you're encountering. How you place and pose your head indicates whether you're being aggressive, flirtatious, or are bored to distraction.

Head movements have many purposes. They can reveal attitudes, replace the spoken word, and support or challenge what is said. You can steer someone to look or move in a specific direction by using your head to guide her, or you can point with your head when finger pointing would be rude or inappropriate.

Slight head nods, chin thrusts, and sweeping actions emphasise words and phrases. In a meeting the chairperson nods or her head to indicate who may speak next.

Discover in this chapter how a slight shift in action or angle can make the difference between being perceived as interested or dismissive, thoughtful or arrogant, playful or angry.

Demonstrating Power and Authority

Power is, indeed, a heady thing, and people with power, whether they're aware of it or not, position their heads in ways that reinforce that power. Particular positions of the head correspond to the kind of power you hold. Lift your head and tilt it backward, and you convey a sense of superiority (and people perceive you as haughty); raise your head and thrust your chin forward, and you send out a 'Don't mess with me!' signal. The following sections explain the variety of messages that head positions signal.

The way you hold your body can cause positive or negative feelings in those around you. Make sure that your head position reflects the response you want.

Signalling superiority

So, you've recently been appointed president of your company, club, or choral society. Had you been paying attention, upon hearing the news you would have noticed that your head lifted when your name was announced. Already, you began to take on the behaviour of a person in a position of authority.

Although you may say that all humans are created equal, when you're in charge, your body sends out signals indicating that you're the one people ought to notice. Sure, you may choose to drop your head in a moment of thought or as a sign of respect, or even to demonstrate a moment of humbleness, but when you want people to pay attention and focus on you, your head rises.

If you find yourself feeling blue, down in the dumps, or just not quite on top of your game, raise your head and hold it in an upright position for a few moments. Notice your mood shifting from low to high. If you're feeling really down it may take a few extra moments to feel the change. Don't lower your head until you notice the difference in your feelings.

Demonstrating arrogance

A difference exists in a look between authority and arrogance, and that difference reveals itself in the tilt of the head and the jut of the chin. Although authority conveys itself with a raised head, arrogance is signalled by a slight backward tilt of the raised head and a forward thrust of the jaw (see Figure 3-1).

Figure 3-1: Arrogance can be conveyed by the head tilt and jaw thrust.

Occasionally, what appears to be arrogance isn't arrogance at all, but camouflaged insecurity. If someone tilts her head away from you slightly, so that she looks downwards over her shoulder, she's put up an invisible barrier between you and her. Although the look of raised head, forward thrusting chin, tilted angle, and downward gaze implies arrogance, the underlying message is one of defensive posturing.

Alex is a solicitor at a top law firm. He was recently put up for partnership, but was unsuccessful. The partners told him that he came across as arrogant and aggressive. Although I thought these were natural traits of a lawyer the partners felt that his body language put people off. On first glance, Alex's behaviour can be perceived as arrogant. He often lifts his head, juts out his chin, slightly turns away from you when he speaks, frequently crosses his arms over his chest, and when challenged adds what sounds like a sarcastic laugh to the ends of his sentences. These behaviours create an impression of arrogance and aggressive superiority that make others feel uncomfortable and threatened. What those of us who know him well recognise is that these actions are covering up a lot of insecurity. His lack of body awareness combined with his self-doubt is sending out negative messages.

Displaying aggression

If someone approaches you in an aggressive state you may notice, if you have the time and the courage, that the head is thrust forward from the shoulders as if it were a weapon. In extreme cases, someone who's really angry may use the head as a missile, projecting it forward in a head butt to hit the other person – a not uncommon behaviour among professional soccer players.

George was leisurely driving along a narrow country lane when from behind a speeding BMW came careering around a corner and almost rear-ended him. Experiencing a combination of fear, anger, and moral outrage George stopped his car, forcing the other driver to brake hard to avoid running into him. The driver leapt out of his car and approached George who wisely stayed in his. In a flash, George noticed that the other man's face was red with anger, his fists were clenched in front of him, and his head was jutting forward from his shoulders, neck sinews extended, jaw tight, lip snarled, and teeth clenched. Wisely George recognised the signs of extreme aggression, kept his windows up, locked the doors, and called 999.

Showing disapproval

Remember when you were called into the head teacher's office and you knew it wasn't because you had won the citizenship prize? Or, perhaps more recently when your boss summoned you to inquire why you hadn't met your monthly target? Or that time your tennis partner threw you a look after you hit the ball into the net to lose the final point in the club tennis tournament? We've all been at the receiving end of the disapproving look. My children assure me that often I'm the one giving the look, too.

As with all gestures, the disapproving look involves several actions. In terms of where you place your head, it's positioned with the forehead slanting forward and the head lowered, as shown in Figure 3-2.

Figure 3-2: A forward tilting forehead implies a critical attitude.

The other head position for showing disapproval is with the head held firmly upright over a straight body. The arms are folded, legs crossed, and the eyes probably looking at you with an icy stare.

If you want to indicate that you're disappointed, critical, or disapproving, adopt a still posture with your head firmly positioned in an upright angle looking the other person squarely in the eye as if to say, 'There's no room for argument or excuses here.' Another position you can assume is to lower your head, stare at the floor, and pick at your clothes with your thumb and index finger as if removing an invisible bit of fluff. These positions reveal that you're harbouring unspoken objections.

To read body language accurately you must observe all the gestures a person is making. The full message lies in the combination of actions, not in a single movement.

Conveying rejection

The head shake is the most common way to express a negative reaction. Infants rejecting the breast, bottle, or a spoonful of food turn their heads rapidly from side to side. Anthropologists believe that for adults, the action of turning the head horizontally from left to right with equal emphasis on each side to express rejection, stems from our earliest days.

The head shake has two speeds of delivery:

- ✔ **Fast:** If the listener shakes her head rapidly she's saying that she disagrees and wants to take over the speaker's role.
- ✔ **Slow:** A slow back and forth sideways turning indicates the listener's incredulity at what she's just heard. The slow shake implies that the listener is comfortable in her position and doesn't want to take over from the speaker.

Catapulting for intimidation

In any business environment you're bound to see someone sitting at her desk, hands clasped behind her head, elbows pulled back, chest puffed out. Whoever takes on this pose immediately increases her size and takes on a threatening appearance. As a gesture, the catapult is a clever way of disguising aggression and intimidation.

Choose your gestures carefully. If your boss calls you into her office to have a word with you, leave your catapult outside unless you're prepared for a counter-attack.

Tossing your head in defiance

A woman frequently tosses her head to show disdain or haughtiness. She flicks her head backwards and gives it a small shake indicating that she has no intention of engaging with the other person, no interest in what's being said, or is unwilling to commit in any way. A person intent on delivering a double-punch gibe holds her head high and throws it back as she lays on the verbal charge.

Beckoning with your head

When you want to attract someone's attention, be it a potential lover, or a helping hand, and a shout or even a wave would be an unsuitable choice, the head beckon is an effective gesture. This head movement is a diagonal backwards throw and may be repeated several times depending on how urgent your request is.

Touching someone on the head

The head is the most sensitive and vulnerable part of the body: It is where the most important sense organs are stored. The hand is the part of the body that can cause the most harm to another person. The act of touching another person on her head is an intimate gesture, implying trust and a deep bond between the two people. If you touch someone on her head you're demonstrating your power over her. Seldom, if ever, would you see a student put her hand on the head teacher's head, any more than you'd put your hand on your boss's head. The person in the position of authority, be she taller, older, or wiser than you, has implicit permission to place her hand on your head.

Priests, Rabbis, and other heads of religious organisations place their hand on a supplicant's head as a sign of divine power.

Kissing another person on her head is a way of demonstrating approval and showing a protective attitude. Because the gesture is a one-sided way of kissing someone it implies that the initiator has a superior position to the receiver.

Showing Agreement and Encouragement: The Nod

An almost universal gesture and the most frequent and obvious head movement is the nod. This seemingly simple action has a variety of meanings. In addition to being a sign of affirmation, agreement, acknowledgement, and approval, this up-and-down movement serves as a gesture of recognition, comprehension, encouragement, and understanding.

Body language is an outward manifestation of your feelings and emotions, or, in layperson's terms, your body is reflecting what's going on inside. For example, if you're feeling upbeat and positive your head naturally nods as you speak.

If you want to establish an affirmative environment but you're not feeling quite so perky, nod your head intentionally and lo and behold, you start feeling on top of the world. Simply stated, if you consciously nod your head you create positive feelings. It's all about cause and effect.

Head nodding is catchy. If you nod your head at someone she usually nods in return. This is true even if the other person doesn't agree with what you're saying. And as for creating rapport, gaining agreement, and getting support, the head nod is your entry point.

Encouraging the speaker to continue

As a listener's gesture, the nod plays an integral part in keeping the conversation going. By using a measured nod, the listener indicates that she's paying attention and doesn't want to take over the speaker's role. This slow, rhythmic nodding encourages the speaker to say more and talk longer. Likewise, by failing to nod your head while listening, the speaker thinks you aren't interested or paying attention. She finds it difficult to continue and quickly ends the conversation.

Start a conversation with someone you know well. As she speaks, nod your head in encouragement. See what effect your head movements have. Then stop nodding all together and observe her reactions.

Showing understanding

Although the slow head nod encourages the speaker to continue, shifting gears and speeding up your nodding indicates that you understand what she's saying. The fast head nod has a certain amount of urgency attached to it and shows that you completely support what the speaker's saying, or that you want to interject and take over the speaker's role.

The way you can tell the difference between someone who's interested and encouraging as opposed to someone who wants to take over the conversation is by observing where she's looking. If the person is looking at the speaker she's being supportive. If she's looking away from the speaker, she's indicating that she wants to take over the conversation (unless she's distracted, of course).

If the listener seems to be looking at the speaker supportively, sneak a peep at her eyes. If they're engaged, she's paying attention. If they're dull, she's probably bored or uninterested.

The strength of the nod – the degree of the up-and-down action – communicates the listener's attitude. If she agrees, the head nod is a firm action. A slight nod provides feedback to the speaker letting her know how well her message is understood.

When making a formal presentation, the head nod is a useful gesture to emphasise words and phrases. Use it wisely. Too much repetition reduces the impact of any emphasising technique.

Micro nodding

Often people end their statements with a barely perceptible dip of the head. In a quick motion the head pulls downward followed by a softer return to the upright position. The action emphasises the speaker's commitment to what has just been said and can be perceived as a slight attack. George W Bush frequently uses this gesture, accompanying his words, 'make no mistake about it'.

Displaying Attention and Interest

If you tilt or cock your head you indicate that you're interested in whatever you're observing. Although men tilt their heads by raising the chin, women prefer the head cock in which the chin is slightly lowered and the head is held at an angle towards the subject of interest.

This section covers all manner of head tilts.

Tilting and canting

Whether you call the action tilting or canting, people and animals incline their heads slightly whenever they hear something that captures their attention. Notice when you perform this gesture that you hold your head at an angle towards whatever's got your interest. The head tilt – or cant – is also used when people are listening attentively.

Although men tilt their heads in an upward movement, mostly as a sign of recognition, women tilt their heads to the side in appeasement and as a playful or flirtatious gesture. When a woman tilts her head she exposes her neck, making herself look more vulnerable and less threatening.

If you're in a social setting and notice a woman in the company of men tilting her head, you can safely bet she's out to gain their attention.

Because the head tilt can be used to indicate that what you're saying needn't be taken too seriously, make sure that when you're making an important point you keep your head upright.

 Fran came home in the wee small hours of the morning after a night out with her girlfriends. Her husband was sitting up in bed, wide awake in a fury. Although she'd done nothing other than have a bit of harmless fun, Fran knew she was in trouble and had to change her husband's mood quickly. She threw herself into her helpless-little-girl behaviour, including wide-open eyes, pouted lips, and canting her head to one side, which she instinctively knew would appeal to her husband's more tender and protective feelings. The gestures worked and after explaining that he had just been worried, and appealing to her to let him know in the future if she was going to be back late, they happily fell to sleep.

 If you want to show that what you're saying isn't meant to be taken too seriously, give a short, sharp downward tilt of your head to one side, and add a wink of the eye. People recognise this multi-purpose gesture as both humorous and conspiratorial, as well as being a friendly social acknowledgement.

The head cock

Cocking your head involves a dip of the forehead and a twist of the chin as you incline your head towards another person. This gesture is frequently used as a non-contact greeting and relates back to the days when men would doff or touch their hats in recognition, or tug their forelocks in acknowledgement of another person.

The head cock is a teasing, cajoling action intended to break down a person's resistance. Women appear appealing and pro-vocative when they employ this gesture, eliciting nurturing and protective feelings from the person they're seeking to entice.

Men who resort to the head cock are seeking sympathy or reassurance, or are showing that they're not the tough, ruthless character they believe that society demands them to be.

The overriding effect of the head cock is of the rush of protective and compassionate feelings. Unless, that is, you know you're being manipulated, in which case you may just feel annoyed.

When you're listening you unconsciously copy the other person's head movements. The empathy that you share with the speaker is reflected in the shared behaviour.

Sitting tête à tête

People who put their heads closely together are showing that a tie exists between them and no room is available for anyone else. The physical closeness reflects their intellectual and emotional bond. The action is one of exclusion and prevents others from overhearing what they're saying.

The next time you're sitting with your friends having a good gossip or sharing a risqué joke, observe how your heads come close together. When the punch line is delivered, or the dénouement of the story is revealed, see how your head positions change.

Indicating Submissiveness or Worry

Charles Darwin concluded that people lower their heads when they're feeling submissive. The act makes a person look smaller and less threatening. If our intention, conscious or not, is to appear compliant, dipping, tilting, canting, and cocking the head all do the job. Research also shows that self-touching gestures, such as holding your head at the back of your neck and placing your hands on top of your head like a helmet, provide comfort, reassurance, protection, and help to alleviate your stress.

Dipping and ducking

If you've ever walked between two people who are deep in conversation you may have ducked your head down to keep from invading their space and to apologise for any inconvenience you may have caused.

Some people make a slight involuntary dip of their heads when they approach another person they think is important or if that person's involved in a conversation with someone else.

People who don't care about status distinctions don't usually display submissive gestures. Those who feel they're intruding on important people excuse themselves with a slight dip of the head.

Marsha is an American living in London. She's an active and successful fund raiser for several high-profile aid organisations. In acknowledgement of her contributions to the charity sector she was invited to attend a reception at Buckingham Palace attended by Queen Elizabeth and other high-ranking members of the Royal family. She was told that when she was introduced to the Queen she was expected to make a formal curtsey. Marsha found that expectation difficult to digest. Although she respects the Queen for the service she has shown to her country, she doesn't acknowledge status differentiations and is loath to demonstrate submissiveness to anyone, even the Queen. Although she didn't perform a full curtsey, out of respect she did give a slight head bow when introduced to the Queen.

Cradling for comfort

The memory from our infancy and childhood of being held and comforted during times of distress lingers and lives in our adult lives. The sensation of having the back of the neck supported creates a sense of security. In times of insecurity people can often be observed with their hands holding the back of their necks (see Figure 3-3). Subconsciously, they're protecting themselves from real or imagined threats. This gesture provides comfort and reassurance.

Bob attended an all-day company board meeting during which discussions became heated. At one point during the afternoon he noticed that his chairman sat back in his seat, put his hands behind his head, and began to rub his neck. He then changed positions, moving forward in his chair, rested his elbows on the table, and continued massaging his neck.

After a few moments, he clasped his hands on the table, took a deep breath, and addressed the group with new-found focus and purpose. He seemed to have become re-energised by the few moments of self comfort.

Figure 3-3: The head cradle provides comfort and security.

The head clasp

Wherever the stakes are high, be they on the sporting field, on election night, or on the trading floor of an investment bank, and despair is in the air, you see people clasping their heads as if they're creating a manual crash helmet. The head clasp is a protective gesture in which the hands rise up and cover the top of the head.

Head clasping is a natural response to calamity, real or imagined, and acts as a metaphorical shield, protecting the head from psychological damage.

Showing Boredom

Someone who is bored props her head in her hand. Her eyes droop at half-mast and before you know it she's nodding off. Resting your head in your hand is reminiscent of your childhood, when someone would support your head when you were tired. You rest your head in the palm of your hand because your head feels too heavy to stay upright on its own. Your palm cushions your cheek and your chin drops in a nod. You're usually bored when what you're doing doesn't inspire you or meet your abilities. You may even feel tired and fed up.

Take comfort in knowing that you're not alone if you've ever felt bored. You can recognise the signs of boredom in yourself and others.

Before determining that someone is bored with what you're saying, look into her eyes. If they're bright and alight the person who's resting her head in her hand may be thinking. If the eyes are dull and unblinking, she's probably bored.

Showing You're Deep in Thought

Some of the most misinterpreted gestures are those that demonstrate pensiveness or deep thinking. Auguste Rodin's sculpture, 'The Thinker', is the prototype for the thinking position. The subject has his head resting on his hand and is in a forward leaning position.

Placing your hand on your cheek indicates thought, consideration, or some kind of meditation. If your eyes are active and regularly blink they show that you're considering your options.

The main difference between someone who's thinking and someone who's bored can be detected in the body's energy. A person who's actively engaged in thought shows interest and attentiveness. Her eyes are engaged, she may have one or both hands placed by her head, and her body leans forward.

Resting your head in your hand, out of boredom or interest, requires hand to head contact, which is a reassuring gesture. Whether you're bored or contemplative you subconsciously comfort yourself with this action, stemming back to childhood. When you're bored and when you're thinking your head may rest in your hand or hands. The way of telling the difference in moods is to look at where your eyes are focused, and where your hands and fingers are placed.

Head resting on hand

When a person's thinking she may bring her hand to her face, put her chin into her palm, or extend her index finger up her cheek while her remaining fingers rest below her mouth. This gesture is particular to the evaluation gesture (discussed in Chapter 8) and indicates that the person is thinking about what to do next.

If the person thinking pulls her body back from the other individual her thinking is critical, cynical, or negative in some way towards the person who's speaking.

When I'm invited to speak at seminars and conferences, I can count on at least a third of the audience to sit with their hands to their heads. I can usually tell those who are interested and engaged by the forward lean in their bodies. Those who sit back with their heads resting in their hands are more of the wait-and-see variety, a bit sceptical and in need of further convincing.

Chin stroking

Someone stroking her chin is indicating that she's deep in thought or making an evaluation. In this gesture a person strokes her chin with her thumb and index finger. The index finger may also stroke the upper lip. If a man has a beard, he may even pull on it.

The 18th century actor, Henry Siddons, in his book *Rhetorical Gestures* says, 'This gesture signifies the wise man making a judgment.'

Chapter 4

Facial Expressions

● ●

In This Chapter

▶ Communicating your feelings when words are inappropriate

▶ Recognising facial expressions that reinforce the spoken message

▶ Masking emotions

▶ Expressing a range of emotions

● ●

*F*ace it. No matter what you say, people are going to believe the look on your face rather than what you tell them. Try as you may to hide your feelings, the curl of your lip, the glint in your eye, or the flare of your nostrils gives the game away. Second only to your eyes, your face, when it's moving, is your most expressive feature.

Facial expressions exert a powerful control over the type and amount of communication between individuals. People make personality and other judgements about each other based on what they see on their faces. Rightly or wrongly, people believe that someone with an attractive face has many other positive attributes.

Sometimes letting your expression do the talking is more appropriate than blurting out what you're thinking or feeling. At other times you may need to reinforce your spoken message with a physical gesture, or express emotions when words fail you. Here's where your face comes in handy.

Communicating Feelings When Words Are Inappropriate

Take a healthy measure of lips, teeth, jaws, cheeks, and you can create yourself a plethora of facial expressions. With more than 44 muscles in your face – 22 per side – you can communicate just about anything you want simply by look alone. And sometimes a look is all you need.

Say that you think the person sitting across from you is attractive, but you'd feel a fool coming out and saying so. The other person may feel a bit threatened or uncomfortable if you expressed your feelings out loud. So, what to do? You establish eye contact and hold it a little longer than usual, you give a little smile, and if you're a woman you may drop your chin a fraction and look up from under your eyebrows. If you're a man you probably tilt your head back. Not a word's been spoken, yet a frisson is in the air.

You may want to send a message telling someone that his behaviour isn't acceptable. A lowered brow, tightened lips, and a slight shake of the head are usually enough to make your point.

A disapproving look may not always be enough. William was a 4-year-old pageboy at his uncle's wedding. William's mother was seated near enough to her son to catch his eye, but not near enough to grab his hand. During the ceremony William became fractious and began playing with the other young attendants, in spite of his mother's attempts to control his behaviour with her facial signals. No matter how much she frowned, put her index finger to her pursed lips while shaking her head in a definite, 'No' gesture, William took no notice. Finally, he turned his head sharply in the direction of his mother, frowned for all he was worth, and made a face at her – his little way of saying, 'I know what you want and I'm going to do this my way!'

The next time you disagree with your boss, partner, or associate and believe that it would be inappropriate to say so out loud, you can engage the other person in a bit of ocular one-upmanship. Hold the person's gaze slightly longer than you would normally, with your lips tightly closed. If your timing's right your expression states your position without saying a word.

Recognising Facial Expressions that Reinforce the Spoken Message

As with all gestures, what your face reveals is going to be believed more than the words you say. Flash your eyebrows in recognition of someone whose company you enjoy, frown when reading your child's school report, smile as a loved one approaches you, and your facial expressions match your verbal message.

Tell your daughter-in-law how happy you are to see her while your facial expression says that you've been sucking on a lemon or you've been frozen in cold water, and don't be surprised if she holds back from you.

Open facial gestures – in which your eyes are engaged, your mouth is relaxed, and your head is tilted with interest – are safe and inviting. Working in combination with positive language and a well-modulated voice, your facial gestures confirm the spoken message. When you're speaking or listening and you want to indicate that you're open to the other person and are prepared to give him a chance, make sure that your facial expressions are open and match your verbal expressions. Conflicting gestures send mixed messages.

To develop a well-modulated voice that represents you at your best, start by breathing correctly. Allow yourself to breathe from your abdomen, like a newborn baby. After you've mastered that technique, begin to hum to relax and develop your vocal chords. A well-modulated voice resonates and rises from a firm foundation.

Myles's girlfriend, Laura, lives near Manchester and Myles lives in London. Because of the distance between the two cities, Laura stays for several days when she visits Myles, who lives at home with his mother, Tina. Tina thinks Laura is a pleasant girl and appreciates the care and attention she's shown Myles. Since they've been dating, Myles's self-confidence has grown and Tina acknowledges that Laura is largely responsible for that. However, Tina doesn't like Laura's over-dependence on Myles and the lack of initiative she demonstrates when she's visiting. Tina initiates the conversations and asks Laura for her help when she's getting dinner on the table. Laura has a bit of a whine in her voice, which Tina also finds annoying. Laura told Myles that she didn't think his mother liked her. Although Tina does like certain aspects of Laura's personality, there are parts that she doesn't. Tina thought that she was demonstrating openness in the way she engaged with Laura. What she didn't realise was that her facial expressions weren't as open as she believed and Laura was picking up on that.

Suri was scolding her young son, Jordan, for drawing a rainbow on the newly hung wallpaper. Jordan looked scared when his mother first called his name. His lips trembled, and his eyes were wide with fear. After a moment he relaxed. Although his mother was frowning at him, her mouth looked liked it was smiling. After being told not to draw on the wallpaper again, Jordan skipped off. While Suri was initially annoyed when she saw Jordan's crayon drawing, she also thought it was quite sweet.

Because of the powerful impressions non-verbal behaviour can make, choose those gestures that represent the message you want to convey.

Bill Clinton is known for his powers of persuasion. A technique he employs with alacrity is interspersing his remarks with a wide range of facial gestures. During the Labour Party Conference in Blackpool in October 2002, Clinton was called in to convince the non-believers that Britain must support the United States in war against Iraq should the necessity rise. A master of the gesture, Clinton utilised his knowledge of theatre, people and persuasion to act out his feelings. Notably, he used the 'lower lip bite' to create the impression that he connected deeply with his audience and experienced their fear and pain.

When you're not being perceived the way you want to be, consider your facial expressions. If your face is saying one thing and you mean something else, you may have to change your expression. To counteract the message that your non-verbal behaviour projects, readjust your behaviour.

Masking Emotions

If you've ever bitten your lips to keep from blurting out sentiments that would undoubtedly cause offence, if you've ever smiled when your heart was breaking, or if you've ever frowned when you've wanted to laugh, you know what masking emotions is all about.

When people want to avoid expressing what's going on inside, they create the opposite facial expression with their pliable facial muscles and skin, and hey presto! they're masking their emotions.

I recently attended a luncheon party and sat across the table from a woman whose mother had died two days previously. Before eating, the guests were asked for a moment of silence in memory of Dottie. I was fond of Dottie and was saddened to hear of her death. I looked at her daughter, whom I didn't know, and as we caught each other's eyes we exchanged poignant smiles. Anyone watching would have seen that we both held our mouths tightly with no showing of teeth – hers slightly pulled to the side, mine more a straight line – our eyebrows tense across our foreheads, and we gave each other slight head nods for fear that doing more would allow the sense of loss to come flooding forth. Although we were doing our best to cover our sadness, a careful observer would have noticed the struggle it took to maintain the mask.

After the Falklands War the then British Prime Minister, Margaret Thatcher, was interviewed on television and asked why a British submarine had been instructed to torpedo the Argentine battleship, the *Belgrano*. Purportedly annoyed that she had to undergo the journalist's questioning, and knowing that it was important for her career that she was seen as informed, calm, and in control, she explained that because the ship was inside the British exclusion zone the action was justifiable. Both she and the journalist knew that was a lie. The truth was that the ship was sailing away from the Falklands and was outside the exclusion zone when attacked. While Mrs Thatcher was making her false reply, her mask fell for a split second and she revealed a brief expression of anger. She gave a quick smile, which anyone looking carefully could detect was false from the lack of engagement in her eyes followed by a momentary flash of anger. Her eyes protruded and her jaw thrust forward. As quickly as the expression appeared it was replaced by her masked expression.

A jutted jaw and protruding eyes indicate anger or annoyance.

Expressing a Range of Emotions

Gestures reveal attitudes and emotions whereas words reveal information, and the range of emotions people experience on a daily basis is vast. From anger to worry, you can count on your face to reflect your feelings.

Showing happiness

If your grandmother was anything like mine, she'd tell you to 'put on your happy face' when meeting someone new because she knew, intuitively, that people respond positively to positive behaviour.

Facial displays of genuine, unadulterated, free-flowing happiness can't be missed (see Figure 4-1). When you're experiencing pure joy your eyes involuntarily twinkle, the laugh lines at the outside corners of your eyes deepen, your cheeks raise, and as your lips pull up at the sides and separate you expose your pearly white teeth. No one can doubt your joy.

Insincere smiles are easily spotted. You need more than pulled back lips showing off your pearly whites to convince someone that you're feeling happy, pleased, or any other positive emotion. If your eyes aren't engaged with your mouth – that is, if your lips pull back in a smile and your eyes are dull, listless, or averting the other person's gaze – you're sure to be spotted as insincere.

The fake smile, like the one in Figure 4-2, looks manufactured and unnatural.

Find another word to replace 'Cheese' when you're taking someone's photograph and you want him to smile. This word pulls back the zygomatic major muscles resulting in a false smile and an artificial-looking photo.

Figure 4-1: A genuine smile pulls back both the mouth and the eyes.

Figure 4-2: Insincere people use only their mouths when smiling.

If you're with someone who smiles at you and says he's happy, but a little voice inside tells you that something's amiss, listen to the voice. Look at the eyes and the cheeks for confirmation. To spot a genuine smile, look at the fleshy part of the eye between the brow and the eyelid. If it moves downwards and the end of the eyebrows dip slightly, the smile is for real.

You can tolerate a lot of awkwardness in another person if he shows by his facial expression that he doesn't purposely want to be difficult without a good reason. By showing that he's doing his best to be amiable in the circumstances, his behaviour becomes more acceptable than in someone who's disagreeable in both behaviour and style.

Cecilia had a noon meeting with a potential new client. Her train into Paddington was delayed and she had to rush to catch her tube. When she exited at the right station, she was unable to find the building. Cecilia prides herself on her punctuality and began to worry that she was going to be late. She saw two men walking briskly toward her. From the pace of their stride, it was clear they were focused on where they were going. Cecilia, appreciating their needs, walked towards them with a mixed look of openness, concern, and confusion on her face, making clear that she was a nice person in need of help. She matched the men's pace, apologised for interrupting them, and asked if they were familiar with the area, which they were. When she first approached the men, she noticed a momentary flicker of annoyance cross their faces. She kept her expression open, matched their walking pace so as not to slow them down, and thanked them politely and with another smile when they pointed her in the right direction.

Revealing sadness

Look at someone who's feeling blue and you can see that his facial features are slack and sagging. His eyes are dull and lifeless and the sides of his mouth are probably cast downward. His face seems to have melted or collapsed.

Lips frequently tremble when someone experiences feelings of grief or sorrow. His eyes may become moist, and often a person in this position covers his face with his hand as if blocking out whatever is causing him to feel sad.

Demonstrating disgust and contempt

Disgust and contempt can be shown in varying degrees, but the general look involves the mouth grimacing while the eyes narrow. The nose wrinkles, the chin drops or lifts a fraction, and the head turns slightly to the side.

Chappy and her mother Jean were having a heated political discussion. Not surprisingly, Chappy's views were in direct opposition to those of her mother. Finally, unable to win the argument or to convince her daughter of her misguided judgement, Jean, in a high display of contempt, wrinkled her nose, narrowed her eyes, tightened her lips, and shook her head in disgust as if she had just smelt an over-ripe Gorgonzola.

Signs of contempt are common in the business environment. Looks of disdain and scorn are tossed about the office floor with regularity as when one high-flyer attempts to dispose another.

Nicola is extremely talented at spotting new trends in consumer behaviour. Although her boss admires her perception she also feels threatened by Nicola's youth, energy, and ability to engage with senior board members. During meetings Nicola's boss often responds to Nicola's observations and recommendations with pursed lips, a slight narrowing of the eyes, and a small turn of the head away from Nicola, as she attempts to engage with a senior member of the team to dismiss Nicola's contribution.

Showing anger

You've experienced the emotion, you know the feeling, and you've worn the expression. Anyone in your vicinity recognises the signs. Before the big blow up you probably stare hard at the source of offence without flinching. Your eyebrows pull down and inward, causing your forehead to furrow. Your lips tighten and turn down at the corners, or open stiffly as if in a frozen shout. You may also grit your teeth together. Some people flare their nostrils when enraged. Finally, if you're incandescent with rage, your face can turn white as the blood drains from the epidermis.

If your anger is about to get the better of you, breathe deeply from your abdomen. Inhale deeply through your nose, hold for a moment, and exhale slowly through your mouth. Deep breathing provides oxygen to the brain and you can think more clearly. The time it takes for you to breathe and exhale gives you a moment to reflect and calm down.

Recognising surprise and revealing fear

Expressions of surprise and fear are closely connected. In both expressions, the eyes widen and the mouth is opened. The differences are subtle and found primarily in the attitudinal shape and position of the eyebrows, eyes, and mouth. A few other telltale differences can also be picked up.

Surprise!

An expression of surprise, unlike a fearful expression, is open and colourful. From the whites of your eyes and teeth to the redness of the inside of your lips and your mouth, which you expose as your jaw drops, a person can tell when you're genuinely surprised. Granted, not all people open their mouths, but the whites of the eyes show, and the eyebrows rise in an arched position.

Justin and Sylvia secretly wed, with only the priest and two attendants present. They hadn't been dating long and few of their friends expected them to last as a couple. When they invited some of their friends to dinner and told them what they'd done, their guests raised their eyebrows and dropped their jaws in surprise, never having expected to hear that news.

When you're surprised or startled your eyebrows shoot up in an arch and, horizontal wrinkles appear across your forehead. The whites of your eyes become more noticeable as you widen your eyes and your jaw drops, leaving your mouth in a slack position.

You may notice that someone who has been genuinely surprised covers his mouth with his hand. This is an example of holding back an extreme emotion. Go to Chapter 8 for more information on how revelatory hand movements can be.

Boo!

The telltale signs of a fearful expression are

- ✔ A tensely pulled back open mouth
- ✔ Raised eyelids
- ✔ Exposed whites of eyes

When you're full of fear your eyebrows rise and pull together in a crooked curve. The centre part of your forehead wrinkles and, while your upper eyelids rise exposing the whites of your eyes, your lower eyelids become tense and rise, too. Finally, your lips tense and may pull back around your open mouth (see Figure 4-3).

Figure 4-3: A fearful person's face is tense.

Demonstrating interest

When showing interest in what someone is doing or saying you may find yourself cocking your head in his direction and nodding in agreement. Your eyes widen, taking in the information and your mouth may be slightly opened.

The open position indicates interest. Whether the interest is romantic, intellectual, spiritual, or just plain friendly, the look on the person's face is open. The eyes are engaged, the head may tilt or nod, and the body leans forward as if getting immersed in the subject. No blocks – such as lowered eyebrows, a jutting chin, or a furrowed forehead – stand between you and the person you're interacting with. You lean forward, ready to go, and your expectant face follows.

People nod when they're listening. A slow nod shows that they're taking in what the other person's saying and are prepared to let him continue. A fast nod indicates that although the person may be interested in what the speaker's saying, he feels a sense to hurry things along.

Research into the behavioural similarities within the animal kingdom shows that birds, dogs, and humans amongst others cock their heads when they're listening attentively. So if you want to know whether your dog or parrot's paying attention, look to the tilt of his head.

When evaluating what you're observing, you may raise one hand to your cheek with your index finger pointing upward and your thumb supporting your chin while your other three fingers curl in on your palm. When decision time arrives, you and your colleagues may find yourselves stroking your chins in a sign of thoughtfulness and contemplation. (Go to Chapter 8 to find out more about what hand gestures mean.)

Chapter 5

The Eyes Have It

*B*ecause much of our face-to-face time with people is spent looking at their faces, the signals they send out with their eyes play a vital part in revealing their thoughts and attitudes. In fact, of all our body language signals, the eyes reveal our thoughts and emotions most accurately: They're placed in the strongest focal position on the body, and because the pupils respond unconsciously to stimuli they can't be artificially manipulated or controlled (well, you can artificially increase pupil size with belladonna but that's going a bit far).

Your eyes are the gateway to the soul and reflect what's going on inside of you. They're also the means of seeing what's going on inside of someone else. Some people instinctively know how to use their eyes to their own advantage, to garner sympathy, convey sexual interest, or to deliver the message, 'Stay away!' With practice, your eyes can speak the messages you mustn't say aloud. This chapter looks at the role that eyes play in communicating your feelings and intentions. You discover how to use your eyes to command attention, display interest, show disapproval, create intimate feelings, and demonstrate dominance. And because communication – even with eyes – is a two-way street, I tell you how to read the eye signals that others give you.

The Power of the Held Gaze

Establishing and maintaining eye contact comfortably with another person can be the basis for successful communication, giving you and the person you're communicating with a feeling of wellbeing and trust. But sometimes, eye contact can be uncomfortable, such as when the other person seems dishonest, untrustworthy, or angry. Whether the interaction is comfortable or not has to do, in part, with the way that a person looks, or doesn't look, at you. The intensity and length of time she holds your eye influences the meaning of the gaze. The following sections explain the different attitudes that a held gaze can mean.

Jennifer is a psychiatric doctor working in private practice. A patient of hers, Dorothy, is an elderly woman who was diagnosed schizophrenic when she was in her late teens. Dorothy has managed to live an active life through the use of medication and psychiatric treatment and many of her friends aren't aware of her illness. One behaviour that Jennifer noticed about Dorothy is the way she stares at another person for long periods of time without speaking. The look is difficult to read because of the blankness of the stare. The look is unflinching and can be unnerving to people who aren't aware of the problem.

When a person holds your gaze she's telling you one of two things: She finds you attractive or interesting, or she may be feeling anger or hostility towards you and is offering you a non-verbal challenge. How do you tell the difference? Look at her pupils: In the first case, the pupils are dilated; in the second, the pupils are constricted.

To show interest

You can demonstrate interest in what you're doing or saying by fixing your gaze directly on the person or object you're addressing for slightly longer than you may normally do. The length and direction of your gaze tells anyone who's paying attention that you only have eyes for who and what you're looking at. The moment you look at another person, you have given that person your attention. Hold the look for more than two to three seconds and you imply that the person has grabbed your interest and has your permission to look back at you.

Lizzie went to an art fair with her friends, Frank and Peter. Their taste in art – South American contemporary with a twist – was very different from Lizzie's, whose preferences tended toward Monet and John Singer Sargent. Lizzie was uninterested in most of the paintings her friends were admiring. Not wanting to appear bored or dismissive of their taste, Lizzie forced herself to look at the paintings for longer than she would normally have done. Not only did Frank and Peter believe that Lizzie was enjoying the art, she discovered that by giving the work extra 'eye time' she began to appreciate it in a way she previously hadn't. Although she didn't want it in her home, she recognised how other people could value it.

In social situations focus your gaze on the triangular area between your listener's eyes and mouth. You're perceived as non-threatening and interested.

Building rapport

When you want to build rapport with someone, research shows that you need to meet that person's gaze between 60–70 per cent of the time. If, for example, Penny likes Tim and wants to do business with him, she should look at him a lot. In response, Tim senses that Penny likes him and likes her in return. They easily look at one another and before you know it the deal's been done!

But what about the shy, timid people who find eye contact difficult? No matter how genuine, honest, and dedicated they are, by struggling to establish and maintain eye contact they send out signals of prevarication and doubt.

Given the choice of working with a person who appears nervous and timid, and who has to make an effort to look at you at all, or Penny with the engaging eye contact who makes you feel good about yourself, which person do you choose? You're probably going to choose the one you have the better rapport with. Even if you feel uncomfortable making eye contact, make the effort. The more you get used to looking another person in the eye the more confident and trustworthy you appear, and the more rewarding your interaction is likely to be.

Ed regularly has to make formal presentations for his work. Although once into the presentation he's able to look at his audience – albeit fleetingly – he finds establishing eye contact during his introduction extremely difficult. By watching himself on video replay he realised how much impact he loses by not making eye contact with his listeners. He recognised that, by failing to establish eye contact with his audience at the very beginning of his presentation, he fails to engage with them and has to work that much harder to gain their attention, interest, and eventual buy-in. To create rapport with his listeners Ed now establishes eye contact with them before he even begins to speak.

Creating intimate feelings

By letting your gaze wander from the receiver's eyes down the face and below the chin to other parts of the body, you're indicating an interest far removed from the world of business or a friendly 'hello'. In allowing your eyes to wander over your target's face and body, you're showing that you're attracted to that person. If the look is returned, you may be onto a winner. If not, revert to the social gaze or else you may find yourself in big trouble.

When a woman finds someone attractive she may give that person a sideways glance with dilated pupils. This is referred to look as a 'come hither' look because it's saying, 'Come and get me.' If she doesn't want to be so obvious she uses the Social Gaze and keeps her target guessing. (For more information on all the uses and meanings of sideways glances, go to the section 'The sideways glance' later in this chapter.)

To show disapproval, disagreement, and other not-so-pleasant feelings

Of course, not all gazes are warm and friendly. Often gaze alone can indicate displeasure. Beady little eyes, snake eyes, and shooting daggers with the eyes are sure signs of disapproval or disagreement. If a person holds your gaze for more than two thirds of the time and the pupils are constricted you can bet you're in disfavour. If, however, you're able to hold the gaze for several seconds longer than you normally would without looking away – an action that would indicate submission – you can send out your own message of disagreement.

Because your pupils contract when you're angry or in a negative mood, the eyes look harsher and less friendly. Fake your smile and backslap all you want, if you're not pleased with what's going on and don't want to give the game away you'd better put on your dark glasses to hide your feelings.

To show dominance

A dominant person is the one with authority. This person takes command, holds the power, and influences others. The dominant person is in charge.

People in positions of dominance use eye contact confidently. Because they're sure of themselves, their eye movements tend to be slow and smooth. They're comfortable looking at another person for an extended period of time, being careful not to stare, which would just make them look slightly mad or rude.

Gazing is done in two ways: away from, and towards. Both types of eye placement can successfully demonstrate dominance. Those in control of the interaction demonstrate their dominance by choosing when and how long to look at the other person. The following sections explain how dominance can be conveyed through the power of the gaze.

If you want to be perceived as dominant, strong, and in control, slightly narrow your eyes. Donald Trump is a master of the beady-eyed glare. So is Anne Robinson in *The Weakest Link*. Throughout his career Clint Eastwood has used this 'visor eyes' posture to great effect most recently in *Million Dollar Baby*.

Scenario 1: Being reprimanded

When you want to make a strong point, deliberately avoid eye contact to raise the other person's anxiety levels. If you've ever been reprimanded by an irate boss or disappointed parent you may recall how the anxiety levels rise when the person speaking refuses to look at you. You know that any moment you're going to get the full force of her glare, it's just a matter of when.

When I was working as a hostess on a cruise ship I was called into the Cruise Director's office early one morning. Scotty was a stickler for punctuality and I had been late for an event the night before. I knew I was in for it because I'd heard him shout at my colleagues on other occasions. What I didn't know was how intense the confrontation would be. When I entered his office he was sitting quietly behind his desk, staring out at the ocean with his back turned to me. With barely a glance in my direction, he told me to sit down. Continuing to look out the porthole he began to berate me not just for the previous night's transgression but for all my other failings as well. Unable to remain quiet and let him blow off some steam I gave him excuses and argued back. Big mistake. He spun around in his seat and fixed me with a glare so forceful that it felt as if I'd been slapped in the face and punched in the chest. His stare was so intense and he held it for so long that I was unable to meet his eyes. Scotty told me that I'd better watch myself and that he was 'keeping an eye' on me. As he said those words I looked up to see his eyes boring directly into mine. Not able to sustain the eye contact I looked away. There was no question at that point who was in the dominant position.

If you find yourself disagreeing with someone and want to make your point, hold the eye contact slightly longer than you would normally. Without saying a word, you leave no doubt that you, too, are feeling dominant and should be taken seriously.

Scenario 2: In conversation

In conversation, the dominant person spends more time looking at the other person when she's talking than when she's listening. Whoever is speaking has control over the interaction. A dominant speaker watches her listeners to make sure that they're paying attention and aren't about to cut in. When the dominant person is in the listening position, however, she conveys her status by reducing the amount of time she spends looking at the speaker indicating that she's not interested in flattering that person and is soon taking back the speaker's role.

Scenario 3: The unflinching stare

You can grab the attention of an adversary by looking her directly in the eye without flinching. Direct eyeball-to-eyeball staring can be deeply threatening. If you've ever played the child's game of stare-you-out you know that at some point you, or your partner, breaks the contact because maintaining it is just too difficult.

My darling mother has an uncanny way of looking at a person straight in the eye without batting an eyelid when she disapproves of what that person's doing. Her mouth tenses, her eyes narrow as they tighten around the edges, and her gaze doesn't falter. My sister, other selected family members, and I have all experienced the stinging effect of this piercing gaze, lovingly referred to as 'The Look.' It is unflinching, judgemental, and can reduce us to responding in one of two ways: We attempt to stare our mother down, which we have yet to achieve, or else, unable to stand the pressure, we avert our eyes in a downward glance. Either way, Mother wins.

If someone's trying to bully you or put you off, look your foe straight in the eye, narrow your eyelids, and focus directly on your target. If other people are around, let your eyes move slowly from one person to the next without blinking. Move your eyes first and let your head follow, keeping your torso still. The effect is unnerving. If you need a role model, Arnold Schwarzenegger in *The Terminator* is your man.

Effective gazes in business situations

If you want to come across as a person to be taken seriously keep your gaze in the triangular area between the eyes and the centre of the forehead. As long as your eyes remain in that space and you keep control of the interaction the other person reckons that you're someone who means business. The following are other tricks that come in handy in business situations.

Controlling a bore

Looking a tedious, dull, and mind-numbing bore straight in the eyes without flinching is a highly effective way of stopping her in her tracks. If you fix your eyes directly in the business gaze triangle without a flicker of an eye you may be amazed at how quickly your bore comes to a halt.

At last, a way to shorten business meetings!

One study showed that in presentations where visual aids are used, 83 per cent of the information is absorbed visually, 11 per cent through the audio channel, and 6 per cent through the other three senses. A study conducted at The Wharton School of the University of Pennsylvania found that in presentations that relied solely on the spoken word only 10 per cent of the information was retained. In order for a verbal presentation to be effective, key points must be repeated frequently. When a visual element is added to a verbal presentation the retention rate increases to 50 per cent. The result is that by using visual aids in your presentations you achieve a 400 per cent increase in efficiency. Further findings showed that when visual aids are used in business meetings, the time of the average meeting is 18.6 minutes as opposed to 25.7 minutes. This equates to a time saving of 28 per cent.

The power lift

If you want to get your message across when you're presenting visual information during a meeting, you have to guide the audience's attention to where you want them to look. A simple way of controlling your listener's attention is to use a pen or pencil. Point to your material and verbalise what you're showing. Then, lift the pen, or pencil, off the page and hold it between your eyes and your listener's (see Figure 5-1). This movement works like a magnet as your listener lifts her head, looks directly at you, and while both hearing and seeing what you're saying, absorbs your message. While you continue to speak, keep the palm of your other hand open.

Figure 5-1: The Power Lift controls where a person looks during a presentation.

The Wandering Eye: Breaking Eye Contact

Avoiding or breaking eye contact can indicate a variety of things. In many instances, it's a sign of submission or discomfort. Although your instinct may be to run away from unpleasant situations or feelings, fleeing in panic isn't really an option in everyday life because as humans, we aim to cooperate. (Unless, of course, the other person is threatening physical violence, in which case you run in the opposite direction as fast as your legs can take you!) On the other hand, at times avoiding someone's gaze gives you a great deal of strength, appeal, and allure. It's all a matter of whose eyes you're avoiding and how you do it that creates the effect and determines the response. The following are the common reasons why humans avoid eye contact, knowingly or not:

✔ **To 'flee' from an encounter:** Evading someone's glance, gaze, or stare is a defensive, protective action. It's a form of fleeing from an interaction that stirs up in you a 'fight or flight' response. When you think you're going to lose – whether it's an argument or gaining someone's attention – you unconsciously withdraw from the encounter by pulling your eyes away.

Looking away from another person, avoiding someone's gaze, and averting your eyes makes you look smaller. People who feel uncomfortable unconsciously make rapid and frequent eye movements, indicating that they'd rather scuttle away than stay where they are.

✔ **As a sign of submission:** When you look away from a person who makes you feel ill at ease you're relinquishing your power and giving it over to that person.

✔ **To avoid confrontation:** As soon as a sign of confrontation appears, anxious people reduce the amount of time they spend looking at the person with whom they're disagreeing. When you're feeling anxious you avoid looking at another person. Your eyes search for escape routes where you can in effect hide from what's going on rather than seek a solution. When it looks as if trouble's brewing between two people and you sense one of them is going to lose, don't be surprised if you see that person avert her gaze to remove the dominant person from sight.

✔ **As a sign of uncomfortable feelings:** People who are feeling ashamed, embarrassed, or sad, deliberately look away.

✔ **To prompt another person's attention:** Pulling your eyes away from someone can show that you're interested in her. This behaviour is part of the flirtation process and encourages the other person to go after you. If you do withdraw your eyes for this purpose make sure that you look back frequently.

The following sections discuss the ways that many people avoid or minimise eye contact and explain what these different manoeuvres mean.

The eye shuttle

When you observe someone flicking her eyes back and forth, you can bet that she's subconsciously looking for an escape route. Notice that although her head remains still her eyes move rapidly from side to side. The action allows the person to take in everything that's going on around her and see where she can reposition herself without obviously giving the game away.

Dwight was at a business event where he saw Frank, a man he had met once before and whom he believed may be a potential client, or at least a valuable contact. Focusing on his own agenda Dwight made a beeline for Frank who was already engaged in conversation with two colleagues. Dwight re-introduced himself and without being invited, joined in the discussion. What he failed to notice were Frank's eyes shuttling back and forth in search of the nearest exit. Although Frank wasn't interested in speaking with Dwight he was a polite guy and didn't want to embarrass Dwight. While he smiled as Dwight regaled the group with stories and remained where he was standing, his eyes didn't connect with Dwight's as they scanned the room. Frank soon spotted another colleague and disengaged himself from the group, leaving his colleagues to deal with Dwight. Dwight never did do business with Frank, or his friends.

The sideways glance

The sideways glance carries several meanings depending on how it's given. It demonstrates interest, uncertainty, or hostility.

When you look at someone out of the corner of your eye and add a slight smile and raise your eyebrows, as shown in Figure 5-2, it would be fair enough for the receiver to think that you're interested in her.

If someone catches your attention and you want to let her know that you think she's quite cute, look at her out of the corner of your eye and slightly raise your eyebrows. This gesture is mostly used by women and communicates interest.

If you've ever spoken to someone who avoids looking at you while shooting glances out of the corner of her eye, she may well not be very interested in you or what you're saying (see Figure 5-3). It may be time for you to change tack in your conversation, or move on.

Figure 5-2: The sideways glance with a smile shows interest.

People tend to look towards things that interest them, and look away from things that don't. Imagine that you're at a party. Your partner has gone to talk to friends, leaving you with the singularly unpleasant host. Try as you may, unless you're very polite and self-disciplined, your eyes stray in the direction of people or places you find more appealing. The brevity of your glances towards your host signals your lack of interest in her.

If, during a conversation, the listener shoots a glance out of the corner of her eye and combines the action with down-turned eyebrows and a furrowed forehead, you can bet that she's harbouring a critical, dismissive, or hostile attitude.

Figure 5-3: The sideways glance away from you can indicate a lack of interest.

The eye dip

Averting your eyes in a downward direction is a deliberate action designed to placate someone in a dominant position as well as an action designed to hide your feelings. In the first instance, by avoiding another person's gaze, you are giving her permission to take the dominant role in the interaction.

Dipping the eyes is also a way of demonstrating the reluctance you may feel from entering into an interaction. By dipping your eyes you're saying, 'If you want to connect with me, you have to make an effort.'

If you think that acting submissively is a weak or negative role to play, reconsider. Acting submissively can often put you in a real position of strength. And it's sometimes the best way to get what you want. Also remember that, in this manoeuvre, you *choose* to relinquish control.

Diana's dipping eyes

Diana, Princess of Wales was exceptionally adept at evoking empathy by dipping her eyes and lowering her head. This gesture is particularly appealing because it makes the eyes appear larger and makes a woman seem innocent and somewhat helpless. Both men and women respond in a protective way as long as they don't think they're being manipulated. Even as a young child Diana used this gesture to good effect. Although initially she may not have been conscious of what she was doing, experience taught her that when she used her eyes in this fashion she engendered her public's empathy.

Other Ways Your Eyes Tell a Tale

Because your eyes reveal your thoughts, feelings, and emotions – and you've got loads of them – they move in lots of different ways to give away what's going on internally.

Winkin' and blinkin'

An engaging way to show a fun and friendly attitude is to wink. Winking also intimates that whatever you're talking about doesn't need to be taken too seriously. People who are sharing a secret also share a conspiratorial wink.

Not all interactions are fun and friendly though, and one clue is how often the participants blink. On average, people blink between six to eight to twenty times per minute, depending on their state of mind and the activity in which they're engaged.

Blinking longer than usual

If you've ever been in conversation with someone who, while speaking, blocks you out by shutting her eyes longer than she normally would, you know how annoying that action can be. Rather than blinking six to eight times per minute, these people close their eyes in an unconscious attempt to remove you from their sight. Some people find that closing their eyes helps them to think, focus, and concentrate on what they're saying. Or, it can be that they're bored by you or just aren't interested in what you're saying. Perhaps they feel superior to you. Hard to believe, I know, but possible. Whatever the reason, it can be interpreted as rude and off-putting.

I was recently running a workshop on, you guessed it, body language. At one point, one of the participants noted that occasionally I closed my eyes longer than I normally did when I was speaking. Until he pointed this out I was unaware of the habit. As I reflected, I noted that I would close my eyes fractionally longer than normal when I was thinking and speaking at the same time, such as when I was coming up with an answer to unanticipated questions. Shutting my eyes subconsciously shut out potential distractions. Now that I'm aware of the behaviour I can consciously control it. I find that, instead of speaking while I'm thinking, looking at the questioner, pausing, and then speaking is a more effective way of communicating with positive impact.

Blinking more often than normal

Many factors influence your blinking rate. When you're excited you blink more than when you're relaxing in front of the television or concentrating at your computer. The main purpose of blinking is to keep the eye surface moist, clean, and healthy. Under normal conditions, the blinking rate is between six to eight blinks per minute. This can increase by four or five times when you're feeling pressure.

Examples of pressures that can cause rapid blinking include the following:

- ✔ **Normal stress.** Sometimes a high blinking rate doesn't mean anything more than that a person is under pressure.

- ✔ **Lying.** When people lie, their energy increases, and when concocting an answer to a difficult question their thinking process speeds up. However, just to confuse you, sometimes liars slow down their blinking rate.

During the Watergate hearings President Nixon's rate of blinking increased measurably whenever he was asked a question he didn't want to answer.

Blinking less frequently than normal

When you're speaking and the listener is staring at you in a zombie-like fashion, you're probably boring her to distraction. A sure sign that you've lost her attention is the infrequency of eye blinks and the dull glaze that comes over her eyes.

Lack of blinking can be a sign of boredom, hostility, or indifference to whatever is happening, but it doesn't have to be. Confident people, for example, establish more and longer eye contact than people who are uncertain or are attempting to hide something. Although they blink less, they come across as interested listeners. (To find out more about how confident people use eye contact, refer to the earlier section 'The Power of the Held Gaze'.)

Lack of blinking can cause your cornea – the clear, thin top layer of the eye – to become dehydrated. Your vision becomes blurry and you don't see as well.

Active eyebrows: The Eyebrow Flash

Since ancient times people have initiated their greetings with the rapid raising and lowering of their eyebrows. Although this action can be so subtle as to be invisible to the naked or untrained eye, the gesture draws attention to the face in order to exchange clear signals of acknowledgement. When you greet another person, you unconsciously raise your eyebrows in recognition.

Except in Japan where the movement is considered rude and has sexual implications, the Eyebrow Flash is universal and is even used by monkeys and apes to express recognition and social greeting. People who don't use the Eyebrow Flash when being introduced can be perceived as potentially aggressive.

Sit in a hotel lobby or at a bar and Eyebrow Flash everyone who passes by. You find that most people return the Flash and smile. Who knows, they may even come over and talk to you.

Raised eyebrows don't always mean recognition, however. They can also mean the following:

- ✔ **Agreement:** When you agree with what someone is saying, you use the same gesture you use when you greet someone, the Eyebrow Flash.

- ✔ **Surprise and fear:** If you're surprised or scared, your eyebrows rise and stay in that position until the moment has passed.

Widening your eyes

The next time you get the chance, take a look at a baby's eyes. Notice that they're disproportionately large relative to the rest of its face. Unconsciously you respond to large eyes in a protective and nurturing manner. Large eyes make a person look more appealing, as any Hollywood starlet knows. Women create the look of submission by plucking their eyebrows to make the eyes appear larger. They then raise their eyebrows and eyelids, an action that particularly appeals to men. When a woman demonstrates submissiveness by widening her eyes no man in her immediate vicinity stands a chance. His brain releases hormones stimulating his desire to protect and defend her.

If you want to appear innocent and attentive, open your eyes larger than their normal size. Unless the person being gazed at is aware of what you're doing, they're charmed by your likable appearance.

My daughter Kristina has big green eyes. And she knows how to use them. I have observed her with her boyfriends, her father, and even her brother and am amazed and impressed at how she naturally and unconsciously uses her eyes to appeal to the men in her life. When she wants help, be it with her homework or getting her car started on a cold winter's morning, she opens her eyes wide, raises her eyebrows, dips her head, and by gosh, she gets what she wants!

You can make your eyes appear larger by raising your brows and lowering your lids, a technique that Marilyn Monroe used to maximum effect. (Sharon Stone's pretty good at adopting this pose, too.) Men would, and still do, go weak at the knees when they look at photos of her with her lowered eyelids and raised eyebrows. People respond to this gesture because by maximising the space between the eyelid and the eyebrow the eyes appear larger, giving an innocent, sexy, and mysterious or secretive look (see Figure 5-4).

Figure 5-4: Raising the brows and lowering the lids shows a promise of things to come.

Flicking, flashing, and fluttering

Fluttering your eyelids is usually associated with flirting, but is also a gesture you may find yourself using when you've been put on the spot and have to come up with a quick answer. Or, it can simply mean that you've got something in your eye causing an irritation, in which case, you probably rub your eye after fluttering for a moment or two. Flashing eyes indicate hot emotions like anger or resentment although if you flash your eyebrows (refer to the preceding section) you're suggesting agreement or interest.

To flick your eyes over a person or an object shows a modicum of interest which, depending on the response of the person or the amount of curiosity you feel for the object, can move into a longer gaze.

Part III
The Trunk: Limbs and Roots

"I don't know, Mona — sometimes I get the feeling you're afraid to get close."

In this part . . .

Here I travel down the body visiting the parts whose movements reflect inner states and create impressions. How you dress, the way you stand, cross your arms, bite your nails, shake hands with someone – all give an insight into how you feel and, indeed, what sort of person you are.

Chapter 6

Take It From the Torso

● ●

In This Chapter

▶ Recognising how your body speaks for you

▶ Finding ways to change your attitude

▶ Exploring the effects of posture

● ●

*T*he stance you adopt and the way you position your body reveals how you feel about yourself and others. Slumping into your hips, drooping your shoulders, and letting your stomach hang out isn't a particularly pleasing picture and reflects a poor self image. The person who approaches you with head held high, an open chest, and a firm stride is the one who gains your attention.

In this chapter you find out how to get your muscles working with your attitude, to show the world just who you are.

Gaining Insights into the Impact of Posture

How you use and abuse your body determines how you feel about yourself and how others perceive you. Jobs are won and lost, reputations made and destroyed, relationships dissolved and cemented based on how the people involved present themselves.

Walk down the high street on a busy day and observe people passing by. Watch for those who appear to feel good about themselves. You notice that they move with ease. Their gestures are open and welcoming, with shoulders back and heads held high (see Figure 6-1).

Figure 6-1: Upright posture, open arms, and a genuine smile convey ease and confidence.

Keep watching people pass by and notice how the ones who don't seem comfortable with themselves move. Their heads are probably tucked into shoulders, arms folded across chests, and they move at a dreary pace. They look a sad and sorry lot. People who don't feel good about themselves hide in their clothes, their postures droop, and you have little hope of getting a genuine smile from them (see Figure 6-2).

Your posture, gestures, and expressions reveal how you feel about yourself and determine how others relate to you.

Not only can you determine how others perceive you by the way you hold your body, you can also determine your own frame of mind. The way you present yourself reflects and influences your mood and attitude.

Figure 6-2: Depressed posture collapses in on itself.

Evaluating what your own posture says about you

If you spend too much time slouching with a deadpan expression on your face and slumped shoulders you're going to appear inert and ineffectual. If, on the other hand, you hold yourself upright with an alert expression on your face you look energised and ready for action.

To determine what your own posture reveals about your self-image or mood, follow these steps:

1. **Stand in front of a full length mirror and take a good, long look at yourself.**

   Observe how you're standing, the position of your head, and the look on your face. What is the message you're conveying?

2. Turn away for a moment. This time decide how you want to be perceived.

Dominant, submissive, bored, angry, surprised? The list goes on. Carefully consider how you can convey that attitude by the way you stand and breathe, and by the look on your face.

3. Turn back towards the mirror, having adopted the image you want to portray.

What do you notice? What are the differences and similarities between your first and second postures?

By being aware of the messages that your stance, gestures, and expressions send out you can consciously determine how you're perceived. With time and practice you automatically adopt the appropriate pose for the attitude you want to reveal.

Should you find yourself in a downbeat, miserable mood that you want to get out of do the following:

- ✔ Inhale from your abdomen.

- ✔ Gently open your chest as if it were a treasured keepsake.

- ✔ Allow your head to lift from the base of your neck like a balloon tied to a string on a sunny day.

- ✔ Observe your surroundings.

- ✔ Continue to breathe gently, like an infant at rest.

- ✔ Settle into the moment.

If I'm not mistaken, by now you have a gentle smile playing around your lips, and the outer corners of your eyes may even be creasing with enjoyment.

It's okay to not feel good about your body as long as you act as if you do. Why? Because, as I tell my clients, 'The way you act is the way you are.' If you act with a positive frame of mind you feel that way. People want to spend time with you. When you enjoy yourself as you are, you make it easy for others to be in your company. And you may even find that by acting as if you feel good about yourself you find that you actually do.

Showing intensity of feelings

People who are extremely agitated, exceptionally despondent, or enormously cheerful reflect these moods, in part, by the way they hold their bodies. When your feelings are intense it's like putting an exclamation mark at the end of a sentence. Intensity calls attention to itself. For moments of deep despair your muscles relax, your body collapses on itself, and you look like a forlorn rag doll. When you're filled with passion and excitement your muscles tighten, your sinews become taut, and your movements are forceful and concentrated.

Take yourself back to a time when your feelings were working at full tilt. Freeze frame that image of yourself. What do you observe? You see that your muscles are working in equal proportion to your feelings, mood, and attitude.

Signs of emotion being acted out intensely are

- ✔ Fist-slamming
- ✔ Sharp finger pointing/waving/wagging
- ✔ Slouching
- ✔ Stomping
- ✔ Passionate hugging
- ✔ Uncontrollable crying
- ✔ Collapsing from exhaustion

As you read the words you may recognise the feeling. Act out the gesture and the feeling intensifies. Add sound to the action, and the feeling becomes even stronger.

People nodding in agreement, as well as those shaking their heads in disagreement, often vocalise a humming sound. Someone who's annoyed may slam her fist and make a grunting sound as the fist hits the surface.

If you're feeling tired and worn out you may sigh as your body collapses in on itself. If you're feeling energised you may make a short, sharp sound of enjoyment.

If you want to intimidate someone, a low growl in the back of your throat shows that you're prepared to stand up and defend yourself.

At a tennis tournament, my daughter Kristina and I were invited to sit in the sponsor's box. Not only was the seating close enough to observe and enjoy every gesture Rafael Nadal made, we were in prime seats for hearing every thwack and grunt as he and his opponent, Andy Roddick, put their full body force into their swings. As the strokes became stronger, the sounds became louder, and the feelings intensified. We sat forward in our seats and when Nadal eventually won the point, his supporters momentarily lifted themselves from their seats, their hands moving upwards in jubilation as they cheered and clapped. Roddick's camp, on the other hand, dejectedly sat down and backwards in their seats and let out a little grunt-like sigh. Roddick eventually went on to win the game.

If you're cuddling with your honey and want to let him or her know just how much you're enjoying the experience, make a gentle purr or sigh as you snuggle in closer.

Alex was being groomed for partnership at a large city law firm. Although considered to be a bright and capable lawyer, Alex had some unresolved anger issues relating towards his hot-tempered, domineering mother. During a practice role play for his interview, I purposely interrupted him while he was answering a question I'd posed. Angry with the interruption and without thought he rose from his seat and clenched his fists while his facial muscles pulled his lips to a tight thin line (see Figure 6-3). I had no doubt in my mind that Alex didn't like being interrupted. We looked at his actions and decided together that alternative behaviour choices would have worked more to his favour.

Revealing personality and character

Are you King of the Jungle or Misty Milk Maid? Do you see yourself as a winner or a loser? How you hold your body, whether it's upright and crisp or down trodden and limp, shows the world who you think you are.

Figure 6-3: A body's forward and erect posture reveals aggression.

Think of yourself as an iceberg like the one in Figure 6-4. Below the water line is what makes you tick. This inner core contains your sense of self and is the base from which your actions arise. Here you find your values and beliefs, your drivers and motivators, and your strengths and unique selling points (USPs). Above the water line is your outer self, what other people see. The way you gesture, the way you carry yourself, your manners and mannerisms, plus how you choose to dress, reflect how you feel about yourself and all that's going on below the waterline.

If your self-perception is that of a strong, forceful, and dynamic Master of Mayfair your body is upright, your stride purposeful, and your gestures focused and contained. If you see yourself more as a simple, quiet, country lawyer your body may be more relaxed, your way of moving a bit easier, and your gestures more fluid. Whereas if you're Jack the Lad from southeast London, your body may strut and swagger, and your head movements appear quick and sharp.

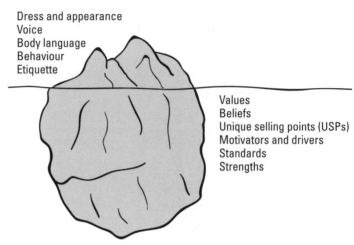

Dress and appearance
Voice
Body language
Behaviour
Etiquette

Values
Beliefs
Unique selling points (USPs)
Motivators and drivers
Standards
Strengths

Figure 6-4: The iceberg reveals the whole you.

If your character has some aspects that you don't like, change your attitude. As your attitude changes so do your actions.

Three Main Types of Posture

Although you have a repertoire of different postures you can adopt, you tend to prefer one to the others. You may prefer to sit, others may prefer to stand, whereas still others are quite happy to spend their time lying down. You can become so associated with one particular posture that people who know you well can recognise you from a distance by the way you use your body. Your posture is a clue to who you are and opens the door to understanding your character and personality.

For example, the person who holds herself erectly has a different temperament from a habitual sloucher.

The three main types of postures are:

- ✔ Standing
- ✔ Sitting (including squatting and kneeling)
- ✔ Reclining

Within this limited list, you can display your mood and temperament by the way you hold yourself and position your head, arms, and legs. People who slouch give the impression of being dull, uninterested, or lacking in confidence. People who hold themselves upright appear to be engaged, energised, and alert.

Standing

Some people are happy to stand. This position enables them to think and move more quickly than if they had to pull themselves out of a chair or get out of bed.

At cocktail parties and other similar events people tend to stand. This enables them to walk towards someone they want to engage with and move away from someone they'd rather not get cornered by.

Because moving toward and away from someone or something is easier from the standing position, it's considered to be a more active position than sitting or lying down.

Participants at meetings frequently stand. The reason for this is that people think more quickly and come to decisions more expediently than they do when given the chance to sit. This is the Let's Go position.

Kate attended a client meeting at an advertising agency in Denmark. When it was time for her and her client to brainstorm some ideas they went to the Stand Up Room, which was designed for quick thinking and decision making. In the middle of the room was a tall stone table, provided for people to lean on and take notes. The table was the only furniture in the room. What Kate found was that, although it wasn't her preferred environment, she was able to make quick decisions and firm commitments.

Sitting

The seated position can be a less energised position than standing. Because your body is bent in the middle, it's easy for you to collapse over your waist or flop back into your chair like a wilted flower if you're feeling a bit tired. Sitting is a more relaxed position than standing. The pressure is taken off your legs and feet and your buttocks take the weight.

Sitting postures convey different states of being depending on how your arms, legs, and head are positioned.

If you're tired you may unconsciously lean back into a chair, letting your legs and arms hang loose with your head tilted backwards. This is a sure sign that you're feeling worn out. At other times you sit upright, ready for action. Your back is straight, you're leaning forward, and you look like you mean business.

If you go into your boss's office and you notice her body's hunched over her desk, wait to be invited before speaking. Her body language is telling you she doesn't want to be interrupted.

Although a relaxed sitting position aids thinking and reflection be careful not to hold the pose for too long. You end up feeling drained and dejected.

The sitting erect position shows that you're focused in the here and now and that you're ready to take a decision or progress an action.

Libby was a focused student, obtaining a First as an under-graduate and further honours as she gained her Masters Degree. She made a point of sitting in the front row during lectures, knowing that there she stood no chance of nodding off or demonstrating any signs of boredom or lack of interest. She says that by placing herself in the front row she was better able to concentrate on what the lecturer was saying.

Lying down

If you want to take some time for quiet contemplation, relaxation, and reflection you may find yourself wanting to lie down. This is the position for getting in touch with your feelings and is a submissive pose. You don't find the prime minister taking this position at a press conference.

As Human Resources director of a large firm, John found himself getting quite agitated before budget reviews, knowing that the partners would challenge him on his training and development expenditures. One quiet afternoon he found himself sitting with his feet on his desk, leaning so far back in his chair that he was almost prone. He felt clear headed, relaxed, and able to sort his feelings from facts. After he made up his mind how he was going to address the partners at the review, and felt confident in his choices, he sat upright in his chair and purposefully wrote his notes.

Changing Attitudes by Changing Posture

If you find yourself in a mood you don't like, change your posture. By changing the position of your body, your frame of mind changes, too. If you find yourself in an enjoyable mood, notice the position of your body as well as your gestures and expressions. By being self-aware you can keep the behaviours you like and eliminate those that you don't.

If you find yourself feeling glum and your slumped shoulders are revealing attitudes you may not want to share with just anybody, physically change your posture and see what happens.

Plant your feet squarely underneath your knees, your knees under your hips, pull up from the waist, and open your chest as if it's a loved book. Let your head rise from your neck and shoulders, floating like a balloon on a string while your arms and hands reach forward as if to embrace

- ✔ A bouquet of your favourite flowers

- ✔ A lover

- ✔ Someone you don't like but have to go through this gesture with regardless

You may have noticed some changes in the way your body moved according to how you felt about what you were embracing. You may have felt mood changes, too.

In addition to changing your posture, you can also use visualisation to galvanise your spirits. To do so, visualise yourself at your most confident. What do you look like? How does your voice sound? What feelings are you experiencing? Notice what's going on around you. If other people are there, what are they doing? How are they reacting to you? Make your visualisation as real as you can. See yourself smiling, your eyes engaged, claiming your space, demonstrating likeability, and moving with purpose. Having created this picture of yourself in your mind you can replicate it any time you're feeling self-conscious, insecure, or lacking in confidence. For further information about visualisation techniques I suggest you refer to *Neuro-linguistic Programming For Dummies* by Kate Burton and Romilla Ready and *Building Confidence For Dummies* by Kate Burton and Brinley Platts (both published by Wiley).

Confident people don't always feel confident. They simply act as if they are.

Using Posture to Aid Communication

I'm not saying that you can tell 100 per cent, exactly, precisely, and without a doubt all the details of what someone is thinking by looking at her posture. What I *am* saying is that you can tell a lot about people's mood, attitude, and state of mind by observing how they hold their bodies. Observing and registering what you notice about how people move and position themselves gives you an insight into how best to communicate with them.

Before beginning an encounter with another person, observe her posture to help you determine how best to engage with her.

Showing high and low status through postural positions

If you think of people in authority you think of them in elevated terms. They don't have to be tall to show that they're top of the pecking order, they just have to carry themselves as if they were. Open and confident posture is the norm for individuals in high status positions. Conversely, people with lower status demonstrate their position by acting in a deferential manner. Their posture is closed and protective.

Indira works for a large city firm. When she was put up for promotion the male partners struggled when making their decision. Although Indira's capabilities were acknowledged as superb, something in her demeanour made them uncomfortable and uncertain. When Indira and I worked on her personal impact, she explained that she had been raised to show deference to people in positions of authority. Because of the hierarchical nature of the firm she saw the partners as authority figures and behaved as she'd been taught. Her shoulders were slightly hunched, her chest somewhat rolled in, and her head slightly bowed. After practising specifically targeted exercises, Indira's posture changed, as did her self-perception. She now stands upright, makes eye contact comfortably, and moves with authority. And, she was made a partner.

The next time you're at an event where people are informally standing and talking in groups, watch the body language to discover who's in and who's out. The people who stand with their weight on one foot are the outsiders, and the ones who lean in with their heads tilted slightly forward are the insiders.

Following are a few random bits of info about posture as a sign of status:

- ✔ When a person deliberately defers to you they are showing low-status behaviour.
- ✔ In many Eastern countries bowing is expected as a sign of respect.
- ✔ In the military a sign of respect is to stand to attention.
- ✔ You're more likely to hold your hands on hips in the presence of individuals whose status is equal to or lower than yours. In front of someone whose status is higher than yours, your body language is symmetrical.

Leaning forward to show interest and liking

According to Professor Albert Mehrabian of UCLA, people who like each other tend to lean in towards one another. The more you like someone, the more your body inclines in her direction. The forward lean is a sign of intimacy and affection.

By leaning towards another person you're sharing space with her and showing that you want to be close. Accomplished interviewers understand the power of getting physically close to the person they're interviewing. After they've created a rapport with the person, they lean towards her to show that there's trust. By appropriately moving into another person's personal space you're demonstrating that you like her.

Debbie and Jonathan have been married for 12 years. They're still physically affectionate with one another and are comfortable cuddling and touching one another. Their friends frequently remark how much physical contact they make and how much in love they seem to be. One Sunday Debbie and Jonathan had a group of friends to lunch. As Jonathan opened a bottle of champagne the liquid spurted from the bottle, making a mess over the counter and floor, wasting half the bottle of bubbly. Debbie immediately rushed to Jonathan and leaned into his chest, giving him a hug with one arm, as she cleaned up the counter with the dishtowel in her other.

Although facial expressions give more information about emotions, posture shows the degree of intensity.

If you carefully observe a group of individuals interacting you can tell their degree of attention, involvement, relative status, and how they feel about one another by the way each one positions her body in relation to the others. People who are actively participating in the exchange lean towards one another. Those who are reflecting on what's going on pull back. The opposite of the forward lean is the backward lean, which indicates fear and displeasure. Someone who's not interested or is bored with the conversation may slump and look in another direction.

If someone is really angry not only does she scowl, she leans forward as well. If someone is filled with happiness she smiles as her body moves forward. It's as if both people want to get further into the emotion. The expressions on the face reveal the emotion. The lean of the body reveals the intensity of the feeling.

Stand upright with your feet hip width apart, put your hands on your hips, lean forward and frown. Now stand in the same position, slightly leaning back and smile. Just by this slight change of posture and facial expression you have conveyed two very different moods.

When you're at a meeting that's lost your interest, sit forward in your seat and rest your elbows on the table while you look at the speaker. This posture both helps your energy rise and you to feel more engaged.

Dicken was preparing for a job interview. He was feeling conflicted about the interview because he was leaving his current job, not having progressed as far in his career there as he'd wanted to. During a practice session he leant back in his chair, letting his chest droop, and his head sink into his shoulders. When he saw himself on video he realised the negative signals he was giving out. I encouraged him to sit towards the front of the chair and lean forward, letting his elbows rest on the table. When he saw himself again, he observed how much more interested, engaged, and likable he seemed.

Shrugging Signals

A child avoiding telling you the truth adopts the wide-eyed, head-pulled-back 'What? Who me?' look as she raises her shoulders in disbelief. The student who's called on by the lecturer to summarise the chapter that hasn't been read, raises her shoulders in submissive apology. The person who wants to show a complete lack of interest gives a disdainful lift of the shoulders as she turns her head away. A submissive gesture, the shrug absolves the shrugger of any responsibility and indicates apology, disbelief, and lack of interest.

Signalling lack of knowledge

You're at your first meeting of the day, feeling confident that you can answer any question your boss may throw your way. And then the unanticipated comes and you freeze like a deer panicking in the headlights. You don't want to show your ignorance so you control your gestures. A well-trained observer, however, would spot the nano-second, micro-movement of your shoulders as your head momentarily drops into your rising shoulders like a turtle sucking its head into its shell.

An elderly couple approached Guy in London to ask him directions to Buckingham Palace. English was not their mother tongue and they struggled to understand Guy as he gave them detailed directions. Looking at them as he spoke, Guy was able to tell that they didn't understand what he was saying. They raised their shoulders and hands in bewilderment as they tilted their heads as if that would help them understand him better. By speaking slowly, using simple terms, pointing in the right direction, and counting out his fingers how long it would take them to get there – if they didn't get lost – he hoped that they understood him correctly. The final lift of the old woman's shoulders indicated that perhaps they had their doubts.

Showing unwillingness to get involved

In addition to conveying misunderstanding, lack of knowledge, and apology, the shrug can also indicate an unwillingness to get involved. Because of the submissive actions that make up a shrug – head pulled down into the shoulders, open forward facing palms serving as a shield, raised eyebrows, and a tilted head – the action indicates that you don't want to be drawn in.

Raising your shoulders is a defensive behaviour designed to protect your neck, one of your body's most vulnerable parts. By holding your open palms in front of you you're showing that although you have nothing to conceal you're also setting up a barrier between you and another person.

Figure 6-5 shows someone who doesn't want to get involved.

Figure 6-5: Forward facing palms serve to push the problem away.

Rory is a secondary school chemistry teacher. Inevitably, at the end of lessons a mess of test tubes, beakers, and other related items wait to be cleaned and put away in their proper place. When he asks his students who's responsible for the mess, without fail they raise their shoulders, palms, and eyebrows as they turn away from Rory, signalling their denial of any responsibility.

If you want to indicate that you want to remain neutral and uninvolved, raise your hand to shoulder height with your palm facing outwards and slightly shrug both shoulders.

Implying a submissive apology

Because the elements in the shrug – hunched shoulders, open palms, raised eye brows, and so on – are all submissive, the shrug is the perfect gesture to use when offering an apology.

A man of few words and the grand gesture, John had been in a foul temper for most of the day. Although Louise is usually quite patient and accepts her husband's moodiness, by late afternoon she was so frustrated that she burst into tears. Realising that he'd been out-of-sorts and treating Louise unfairly, John left the house, returning shortly with a large bouquet of tulips, Louise's favourite flowers. Offering them to her, he apologised without ever saying the words, 'I'm sorry'. The lift of his shoulders, his raised eyebrows, his slightly turned down mouth, and his dropped head as he presented the flowers to Louise conveyed his apology.

Although this exercise doesn't convey emotion, mood, or attitude the shrugging gesture may bring you some relief when you're feeling tense or tired. Raise your shoulders up towards your ears and tighten them as much as you can. Hold that position for three–five seconds, and then release. Roll your shoulders in circles both backwards and forwards to complete the tension release. To avoid injuring yourself when doing this exercise, be careful not to overdo the tightening.

Chapter 7

Arming Yourself

In This Chapter

▶ Shutting people out

▶ Letting someone in

▶ Disguising anxiety

▶ Sending signals through bodily contact

*W*hether you're crossing your arms as a protective shield or opening them as a sign of welcome, the way you position your arms tells an astute observer how you're feeling.

Certain postures elicit certain moods. Crossed arms hold your feelings in and keep other people's out. They show that you've set up roadblocks beyond which no person dares travel. Stay with this position for too long and you find yourself feeling shut off and negative. Unless, of course, you're cold, in which case holding your arms across your chest keeping the warmth in and the cold out makes perfect sense.

As for contact, touching can be a great tonic as long as you know who, when, where, and how. Get touching right and the person you touch feels engaged and connected; get it wrong and prepare yourself for a sharp smack.

This chapter shows you how you can read arms signals, appear self-controlled, and increase your influence through physical contact.

Building Defensive Barriers

Any gesture that protects your body from an assault – be it real or imagined – is a defensive barrier. Ducking your head, averting your body, even tightening your lips and narrowing your eyes, are all examples of defensive behaviours. As opposed to open gestures that welcome others in, these behaviours protect you and keep others out.

Arms crossed on your chest

When you were a small child and feeling threatened and insecure, you may have hidden behind your mother's skirts or a solid piece of furniture. As you reached pre-school age you may have created your own barrier by folding your arms tightly across your chest. During your teen years you probably relaxed your grip and added crossed legs to the equation in order to appear more cool and less obvious.

The crossed-arm position is common throughout the world and communicates a defensive stance. Not only does it serve as a protective guard against a possible attack, crossed arms also represent an inflexible position that tells you that this person's not budging. If a woman finds a man attractive, for example, she keeps her arms in an open position, but she crosses her arms over her chest with men she finds aggressive or unappealing.

You may also cross your arms over your chest if you're feeling anxious, or are lacking confidence. Crossing arms is a common position to adopt when you're amongst strangers and is often seen in lifts, public meetings, when waiting to board an airplane, or anywhere that you may feel insecure, apprehensive, or intimidated.

People who say that they cross their arms over their chests because it's comfortable are right. Any gesture that matches the corresponding attitude feels comfortable. So, if someone feels negative, self-protective, or in any way uneasy, even if he's not consciously aware of these feelings, it is quite common for that person to cross his arms. If he feels relaxed and is enjoying himself, he adopts an opened-arm position that reflects his attitude.

Blocking out information

Two groups of volunteers were asked to participate in an American research project in which the participants attended a series of lectures. The purpose of the project was to examine the effects of the crossed-arm position on retention of information and attitude toward the lecturer. The first group was instructed to sit in a casual, relaxed position, with their arms and legs in an open position. The second group was told to fold their arms tightly across their chests during the lectures. The study showed that the group with the folded arms had a more negative view of both the lectures and the lecturer and retained 38 per cent less information than the group that sat with their arms and legs uncrossed.

The meaning of the message is in the receiver. Studies show that people react negatively to the crossed-arm position. Even if you're comfortable with your arms crossed over your chest, people observing you are going to interpret your attitude as defensive. So, unless you want to show that you disagree or don't want to engage, find other positions for your arms.

If you adopt the crossed arm position when you're in a group of people you soon notice other members of the group adopting the same pose. Although influencing people into assuming this position is easy, you may discover that it's difficult to achieve open communication when the majority of the group has adopted this stance.

Most people adopt the arms-crossed position when they disagree with what's going on around them, as illustrated during a recent public meeting in our village. A landowner applied to the local council to turn his farm into a golf course. The villagers were divided in opinion over this change of land use and a public hearing was held. Those in favour of the change sat on one side of the room while those against the proposal sat on the other. At the start of the meeting many of those who opposed the plan sat with their arms crossed over their chests. As the supporters spoke in favour of the proposal, more and more of the opponents crossed their arms. When the time came for those who opposed the plan to speak, the supporters crossed their arms. As the meeting progressed and people became more adamant and agitated, almost the entire gathering sat with their arms tightly folded across their chests. No constructive discussions took place at that meeting and the individuals present left feeling disgruntled.

An attitude can lead to a gesture or posture that reflects the emotion. As long as you maintain that pose the attitude remains. Therefore, to get someone to change from a crossed-arm position, give him something to do or hold. They he has to unlock his arms and lean towards you. This breaks his negative posture and creates a more open body position, which in turn leads to a more open attitude.

Gripped crossed arms

A sure sign of restrained anxiety and apprehension is when the arms are folded across the chest and the hands are tightly gripping the upper arms. The person appears to be fortifying himself against adversity and holding on for dear life. People waiting in the doctor's or dentist's reception room can often be seen in this position, as can inexperienced air travellers who adopt the posture as the plane takes off and lands, indicating that they are in need of comfort or reassurance.

Depending on their level of concern they may grip their arms so tightly that their fingers and knuckles turn white.

Crossed arms and clenched fists

Cross your arms and clench your fists, and you look as if you're heading towards a fight. This position demonstrates hostility as well as defensiveness, and can lead to aggressive behaviour. Don't be surprised if your jaw clenches and your face goes red too – individual gestures work in combination with others to convey attitudes.

If someone crosses his arms and clenches his fists when you're speaking to him, open your arms and expose your palms in a non-threatening, submissive position. This posture has a calming effect and the other person is more likely to drop his aggressive stance and discuss things in a more reasonable manner.

The crossed-arms, clenched-fists posture is a sign of control and authority. Police officers who cross their arms tend to clench their fists as well to indicate that they're the boss and aren't to be trifled with. Interestingly, people who carry weapons seldom cross their arms because they already feel protected by their weapon.

Crossed arms and thumbs up

A typical pose that superior type, up-and-coming young men adopt when engaging with their manager in the work environment is to stand with their arms crossed over their chests with their thumbs pointing upwards (see Figure 7-1). This position demonstrates both apprehension and confidence. Their uneasiness is conveyed through the crossed arms while the thumbs up position shows self-confidence and a sense of 'coolness' and control.

When you first meet a group of people, you can demonstrate your status and superiority by not folding your arms. Shake hands firmly, stand at the appropriate distance, and keep your hands by your sides or in the power position with one hand resting in the other at waist height.

Figure 7-1: Crossed arms with thumbs up is typical of young, high-flying males.

Richard was recently promoted to partner in a prestigious city law firm. Although considered to be extremely talented and an asset to the firm he also has the reputation of being somewhat brash and arrogant. After shaking hands with the firm's senior partner at a social event for the newly promoted lawyers, Richard folded his arms with both thumbs pointing upward and engaged his boss in conversation. As he spoke he used his thumbs to gesture. This pose showed that while he was seemingly full of self-confidence he also felt the need for some protection.

Because of the structure of women's upper torsos they cross their arms lower on the body than men do. Girls entering puberty tend to adopt this protective position more frequently than more mature females.

Touching yourself: Hugs, strokes, and more

The way you touch yourself gives observers clues as to how you're feeling. Most self-touching movements provide comfort and are the unconscious, mimed gestures of another person's touch, as if you've divided yourself into two people: The one who is providing the comfort, and the receiver of the touch. Some of the more common include the following:

✔ **Hugging or stroking yourself:** When you were a child feeling distressed or upset, your parents, or whoever was looking after you, would hold you in their arms to comfort you. Now that you're an adult, when you feel self-conscious and insecure, and no one's there to reassure you, or it would be inappropriate to seek solace from another person, you hug or stroke yourself to provide your own comfort and reassurance. The most common self-touching actions are rubbing your neck, stroking your arms, or fondling your face.

✔ **Half-hugs:** Because, when you cross both arms across your body, you show that you're feeling afraid or defensive, you may adopt the half-hug position instead. In this position, one arm crosses your body and holds or touches the other arm, creating a partial barrier. Women typically use this gesture more than men.

✔ **The fig leaf:** Men hold hands with themselves in a barrier position to make themselves feel secure. Covering their 'crown jewels' they subconsciously protect themselves from a potential full frontal attack (see Figure 7-2). Look at the line-up of soccer players during a penalty kick and see where they place their hands and arms.

The next time you see someone who's feeling lonely, dejected, or in any way vulnerable, notice how he positions his hands. You see that he holds his hands in the fig-leaf position in an attempt to create feelings of comfort and reassurance.

Figure 7-2: The fig leaf position makes a person feel more secure.

Placing objects in front of yourself

By placing a coffee cup, a clipboard, or any other object between yourself and another person, you are setting up a protective barrier. These barriers are a subconscious effort to conceal any nervousness or insecurity you may be experiencing, whether you're aware of the feeling or not.

During a role play with a client in which she had to enter her boss's office, sit across the table from him, and make a recommendation that she knew he wouldn't like, Lynne clutched a pad of paper in front of her, clasping it tightly to her chest. Although she said that she had to carry the pad for taking notes, the way she held it clearly indicated that she was feeling insecure and threatened. So strong were her subconscious feelings that not even seeing herself on video convinced her that a different posture would create a stronger, more authoritative and professional appearance.

If you're at a function where drinks are being served and you're feeling insecure, hold your glass or cup in front of you with both hands. This action creates a subtle barrier, behind which you can seek refuge. As you look around the room you are likely to see that almost everyone else is standing in the same position, indicating that you're not alone in your feelings.

Giving the cold shoulder

As you are undoubtedly a kind and thoughtful person who would never purposely insult anyone, this section is probably superfluous to your requirements. However, should you ever feel the need to display indifference or aloofness with the intention of giving someone a quick, sharp jab to his ego, turn your shoulder towards him, creating a barrier between yourself and your object of contempt. With a look of disdain, a downward turn of the mouth, and the briefest of glances, the gesture leaves the recipient in no doubt of your feelings of scorn and derision towards him.

Conveying Friendliness and Honesty

Open arms indicate a receptive, friendly, and honest attitude. This position says that you've got nothing to hide and are approachable and amenable. It draws people to you, making them feel comfortable and at ease in your company. By leaving your body exposed you're indicating that you're receptive to whatever comes your way.

Go to any sporting event and watch the players. The moment the winner sinks his final putt, crosses the finish line, or scores the winning goal his arms open with the thrill of victory. The losers cross their arms in front of their bodies or let them hang dejectedly by their sides.

Every summer my son, Max, and I visit his godmother, Libby, who is my dearest lifelong friend. As Libby lives in Oregon and we live in England we seldom see one another more than once a year. The moment Libby sees us exit the customs hall, she flings her arms open before folding us in her embrace. Her open arms are like a welcoming beacon indicating her joy at seeing us.

If you want to persuade someone to your viewpoint, hold your arms in an open position. Open arms indicate a confident, constructive attitude and create a positive impression. You're perceived as sincere, direct, and trustworthy, as long as your other gestures are equally open and forthright.

Touching to Convey Messages

The thing about touching is that it means many things to different people. Touching is a great way to offer comfort, create a bond, and increase your influence. Some people use the gesture as a sign of reassurance, support, and encouragement. Others use it as a signal that they want to interrupt you. Touching frequently occurs when someone's expressing excitement or is feeling festive. You also see people touch one another when there's a disaster or when they're listening to another person's troubles.

The act of touching isn't straightforward. Touch in an appropriate way and you come across as a caring, sharing kind of person. Touch incorrectly and you're perceived as an untrustworthy sleaze. Like most things, it's not what you do, it's how you do it. So heed this advice:

✔ **When to touch:** Neither the United States nor Britain are societies that encourage a vast amount of touching between individuals. People tend to relate a touch to a sexual advance when the intention may simply be to show support, express sympathy, or demonstrate tender feelings. Different people respond differently to touching. Some people are natural touchers and freely give, and comfortably receive, hugs and kisses. For others, unsolicited touching is an anathema and is to be avoided at all costs. If in doubt, don't touch.

Before touching another person pay attention to the kinds of contact he feels comfortable with. Until you know someone well, proceed with caution.

✔ **Where to touch:** A great deal of research has been conducted about where you're allowed to put your hands on another person and where you better not touch. The findings consistently conclude that your opposite-sex friends have more leeway about where they can place their hands on you than your same-sex friends. Unless, that is, you're gay or lesbian, in which case the opposite is true. Mothers are allowed more leeway, but not fathers.

✔ **Where not to touch:** Different cultures have different rules about touching. For example, what you may consider to be an affectionate gesture, such as patting a child on the head or ruffling a friend's hair, is highly insulting in Thailand.

✔ **How long to touch:** Most parents instinctively know long they may touch their children. For example, during a child's infancy both parents are comfortable bathing and changing the child. As the child grows older the father leaves these activities to the mother. This occurs slightly earlier for his daughter than for his son. Eventually, too, the mother leaves her child to bathe alone (and hopes he does a good job of it).

If you're having a conversation with someone who you find appealing, allow your hand to touch his slightly while you speak. Also, when you're introduced and shake hands you may let your hand rest slightly longer in his than you normally would do. If you're uninterested in or are repulsed by the person, your touch is brief and uncommitted.

Touching plays an important part in superstitious rituals. The tradition of touching wood after making a boasting statement stems from the ancient act of touching the sacred oak to appease the god Thor. Touching iron for good luck comes from the archaic belief that iron holds magical and supernatural powers.

Creating a bond

Consciously make physical contact with someone and you immediately establish a connection between the two of you. Parents touch their children, lovers touch their partners, and doctors touch their patients. The power of touch is binding.

Engaging with other people through physical contact is something at which politicians and business people with sophisticated political skills are particularly adept. The double-handed handshake is a favourite of anyone seeking to connect with another person. By using your right hand for shaking and your left hand for touching the other person's hand, lower arm, or elbow, you demonstrate your desire to bond with that person.

The next time you shake hands with someone you've just been introduced to, lightly touch him on his hand or elbow with your left hand as you repeat his name. This creates a positive, memorable impression by making that person feel valued. Plus, repeating the person's name helps you to remember it.

Touching between individuals of equal rank and status occurs regularly. Patting a friend on the back, giving a chum a hug, or squeezing a colleague on the arm, are gestures that convey friendship and camaraderie.

At Hugo's annual rugby dinner the players were jostling about, punching one another on the arm, slapping each other on the back, and draping their arms over each other's shoulders. The young men were comfortable with this level of reciprocal touching between equals. When the coaches spoke to the players they were seen patting the team members on the back, initiating handshakes, and occasionally squeezing their upper arms. At no time did any of the players touch their coaches in a similar fashion. Unconsciously, the players were exercising their symbolic right to impose themselves on one another. In contrast, they demonstrated respect for their coaches' authority by treating them in a different manner.

Get your timing right when touching another person. Holding the touch for longer than three seconds makes the other person wonder what your intentions are.

Save the double-handed handshake and the touching with your non-shaking hand for people of equal or lower status to you. You may be perceived as overly ambitious or familiar if you touch someone with a higher status this way.

The longer the touch, the more intense the message. If you know the person you're speaking to well and you have a good rapport, you can feel comfortable touching that person at length. If you don't know someone very well you're both likely to feel uncomfortable touching. Think of times when you've accidentally brushed up against a stranger or someone you didn't know very well. You probably pulled away quite quickly.

Demonstrating dominance

Something to remember about touching is that it's a hier-archical gesture. The person who initiates the touch holds the authority. The doctor touches the patient, the teacher touches the student, and the priest touches the parishioner. For a person of lower status to initiate touch with someone holding a higher position is considered impertinent.

At his annual summer office party Paul, the chairman of the company, circulated amongst his staff, placing his hand on the shoulders of many of the younger men, and giving the female employees a squeeze on the upper arm in greeting. Not one of the staff members responded in a similar way. Whether they were aware of it or not, they knew it would be inappropriate and impertinent to reciprocate the touch.

Your gender determines, to a large extent, what your touch means. A male boss who touches his female secretary, does so as a sign of power and control. Woe betide the female sub-ordinate who touches her male manager or the female boss who touches her male employee. Whereas a man's touch is perceived as paternal and powerful, a woman's touch is interpreted as a prelude to intimacy with sexual intent. Even in today's world of supposed gender equality, men struggle with the concept of women and power.

Avoid touching work colleagues. Because of laws governing behaviour in the work place you can receive a formal complaint for making a gesture that may be interpreted as inappropriate physical contact.

Research suggests that men perceive women as 'uptight' when they complain about men presumptuously touching them. Female students and women working in restaurants, offices, and factories are used to being touched by their male superiors and they're expected not to interpret these gestures as sexual advances. The research also shows that men may interpret a woman's touch as conveying sexual intent, whether this is the case or not. The findings demonstrate that if touching implies power or intimacy, and women are considered by men to be status inferiors, a woman's touch is read as an intimate gesture, because power is not a reasonable interpretation.

Unless the people who are touching one another are of equal status, the person who is in a higher position is the one who, in theory, initiates the contact. A flagrant disregard for this practice occurred in 1992 when Queen Elizabeth II was visiting Australia. Without considering the potential implications and reactions, Paul Keating, the Australian Prime Minister at that time, put his arm around the Queen's waist in an effort to guide her as she walked amongst the crowds. British traditionalists were appalled at his behaviour. The Australians didn't understand what the palaver was all about. And as for the Queen, we never knew what she thought.

Reinforcing the message

Touch is a powerful gesture. Depending how you administer it, it can be a sign of love, support, anger, or frustration.

Say you're arguing with another person. The tension rises, cruel words are said, and before you know it you're slapped across the face. This is an extreme example of reinforcing a negative message. The gesture supports what's been said and is a physical sign of anger, frustration, and desire to inflict pain.

Your little girl falls down and scrapes her knee. As she cries you cradle her in your arms and stroke her hurt leg to soothe and comfort her. Here, the touch is a calming and placating action meant to reassure and to console.

In both cases the touch reinforced the message. The type of touch determined the type of message being reinforced.

Savvy sales people, marketers, and advertisers understand the importance of appealing to as many senses as possible, including the sense of touch, when selling to the buying public. You *see* the product and your visual sense is stimulated. You *hear* the product, like the snap, crackle, and pop of breakfast cereal or the roar of a powerful engine, and your auditory senses are stirred. And when you *touch* the product, whether soft carpet or smooth leather, your kinaesthetic response reinforces the message that this product is something that you like the feel of.

If you want to appeal to someone, appeal to all his senses.

If you think about it, your skin is your biggest organ. It wraps itself over, under, and all around inside you. Skin is your oldest and most sensitive organ, too. Before you were able to hear or speak you could feel. Your sense of touch began in the womb.

If you're giving advice or information to another person you may touch him on the hand, arm, or shoulder to deepen your connection and reinforce your message.

Before touching another person you need to establish a connection with him. You wouldn't touch a stranger any more than you'd invite a stranger to touch you. In a relationship between two or more people, the dominant person, or the one holding authority, implicitly has the permission to touch.

The mother of the senses

An embryo, rocking in its mother's amniotic fluids, is sensitive to touch. At 9 weeks old, its fingers bend in a gripping motion when its palm is touched. At 12 weeks its fingers and thumb can make a fist. When the embryo's foot is touched on its back or its sole, its toes curl in and fan out.

Notice people travelling in a crowded tube or train. Most draw into themselves to keep from touching the people sitting or standing next to them.

Jo went out to lunch with her friend Caroline who was having problems with her boyfriend. At one point during their conversation Caroline was on the verge of tears. Instinctively, Jo reached out and gently touched Caroline's hand. She let her hand rest there until Caroline composed herself. Jo's touch felt reassuring and had a calming effect. By combining this gesture with a forward lean and speaking sympathetically, Jo was able to help Caroline relax and see things from a more peaceful perspective.

Inappropriately touching another person can be perceived as rude, threatening, and intrusive.

Increasing your influence

Out of your five senses (sight, smell, sound, taste, and touch) your sense of touch is your oldest and most responsive. Your body reacts viscerally to touch, leaning into the hand offering comfort and pulling away from the hand that harms.

If you touch someone on the arm or shoulder when you're asking him a favour, he may well agree. Grab someone by the arm to get his attention and he probably pulls away.

So, how can you tell if someone welcomes touch or is adverse to it? Observe how he relates to other people and objects. People who touch themselves, such as rubbing or stroking their faces, hands, arms, and legs, respond to touch and would probably, all things considered, respond positively to your touch. A person who avoids self-contact and doesn't fiddle with figurines is telling you to keep your hands to yourself.

Wendy wanted her son Todd to agree to follow her into the estate agency business. She hoped that her son would find himself a profitable career selling homes and properties. Todd needed convincing. He felt he didn't have the necessary skills and doubted his ability to close a deal. During their discussion Wendy leaned forward and touched Todd's arm as a gesture of reassurance and gentle persuasion. Her touch felt comforting and Todd's body became less tense. His facial expression softened and eventually Todd agreed to Wendy's plan.

Embracing during greetings and departures

The next time you're at an airport, watch how friends and family members hug when they're arriving and when they're departing. What you notice is that when people hug upon arrival they maintain the embrace longer than upon departure. When they first see one another, the hug is intense and the embrace strong. The people are welcoming and bringing one another into their most personal space. The departure hug is shorter and less passionate. It's almost as though by the time the people are saying good-bye they're having to let each other go.

Part of my duties as on-board hostess for Holland American Cruise Lines was to stand at the gangplank for meeting and greeting of the passengers. At the same spot, a week later, we'd be saying our goodbyes. When the passengers first arrived there was little touching if any between us, as I welcomed them on board. I may have briefly shaken the hands of some. I definitely used my hands to guide others. By the end of the cruise it was a different story. Embraces, hugs, and heartfelt handshakes – we were new best friends united. Having spent days at sea together we had established enough of a relationship to comfortably touch one another. Some I even gave an extra little squeeze.

If someone pats you on the back when you're hugging him, he's giving you a signal that 'enough is enough' and he's ready to be let go of.

Chapter 8

It's in the Palm of Your Hand

. . . .

In This Chapter

▶ Discovering how hand positions indicate attitudes

▶ Making your fingers do the talking

▶ Feeling for different handshakes

▶ Displacement activities

. . . .

Scientific research shows that more nerve connections exist between the hands and the brain than between any other parts of the body. Unconsciously, your hands reveal your attitude towards another person, place, or situation. By the way you position your hands, rub your palms, and fiddle with your fingers you're telling anyone who's paying attention what you're really feeling.

Watch how your hands move spontaneously in greetings, farewells, and as you cement an agreement. Before you know it, your hands illustrate a point you're making and are effective in demonstrating both your sincerity as well as your annoyance. Whether you're expressing love, anger, joy, or frustration, your hands hold the message.

In this chapter you discover how you can use your hands to support the spoken word and add substance to your message. You find out how to position your hands to convey authority and dominance as well as demonstrate openness and submission. You see how other people reinforce what they mean by the way they mimic the actions or situations they're describing. You discover how to read a person by the way she shakes hands, and finally, you discover the telltale signals that the hands and fingers unconsciously reveal when you think no one is watching.

Up or Down: Reading Palms

Numerous experiments have been conducted to record how people respond to hand gestures. Research has shown that when a speaker uses the palm-up position the vast majority of the listeners react positively to what's being said. When the speaker delivers the same message with the palm facing downward the positive response rate drops significantly. And when the speaker points her finger directly at the listener the positive response becomes practically non-existent. The listener reacts negatively toward the speaker, tunes out what she's saying and makes personal judgements about her.

The open palm

The open hand is an ancient sign of trustworthiness. It's a positive position and is helpful for establishing rapport with another person. It is also a submissive, non-threatening gesture. The next time you walk past a pleading street beggar look at how her hand is positioned. Chances are the palm is facing upwards.

Showing honesty

If you want a simple way to tell if someone is being open and honest with you look at where her palms are facing. If one or both of the palms are facing up it's a pretty good sign that you're hearing the truth (see Figure 8-1). When people hold their hands in a front facing open position the words that would match this position would be along the lines of, 'Honestly, I mean what I'm saying. You can absolutely trust that I'm telling you the truth.'

Oh, sure, con artists, professional liars, and used car dealers know the tricks and use the open palm gesture when trying to convince you that they're genuine and sincere. But you're able to detect that something's not quite right because other gestures of honesty, such as open facial expressions, calm breathing, and a relaxed stance, are missing. Alarm bells ring as your instincts cry out, 'Wait a minute. This person's a fraud!'

Figure 8-1: The open palm indicates honesty and trustworthiness.

Making a connection

You often wave to someone you know when seeing her from a distance. Your palm is in the open position, facing front, rhythmically moving from side to side. This is a similar gesture to the one you use when waving good-bye. When you wave it's as if you're reaching out towards that person with a desire to touch her.

A good way to make contact with a large group of people is to hold out one or both of your hands with your fingers spread apart and your palms facing upwards. This gesture, shown in Figure 8-2, acts like a magnet and pulls people towards you.

Figure 8-2: The raised open palm draws your audience in.

When you want to establish a sense of trust and honesty let your hands remain visible. Otherwise, you may look like you're hiding something. (For more information on what hidden hands mean, go to the later section 'Hiding your hands'.)

You can also use open-hand gestures to connect with your listeners, helping them to grasp an idea that you're explaining or showing them that you value their opinions:

- ✔ Say that you want to plant a thought into someone's mind without verbally force-feeding the idea. Bend your elbows at a 90-degree angle and hold out both your hands side by side, as if you're showing her the large size of a fish you've caught. Then slowly beat your open hands rhythmically up and down and watch the light bulb turn on as the listener sees the picture.

- ✔ The next time you're speaking and you want to hear what someone else has to say, turn towards that person with your palm open and extended in her direction. The gesture is as though you're giving her a gift. By handing her the chance to speak, she feels acknowledged and that you're interested in what she has to say.

✔ Watch someone who wants you to come on board with her way of thinking. See if she holds both hands in front with her, palms facing her body as if she's embracing another person. If you find yourself using this gesture when you speak you may also be attempting to grasp your own suggestion or idea.

The downward facing palm

Turn your hand over with your palm facing downwards and Bingo!, you're projecting power and authority (see Figure 8-3). This position is used for giving orders where no room exists for discussion. Gesturing with your palm facing downwards says, 'I'm in control here. Do as I say!'

You have to be careful when using this gesture, especially if your fingers are tightly closed because of its association with dominance and tyranny. Think of the Third Reich and the Nazi salute if you're in doubt. Hitler purposely selected this gesture. He instinctively understood the intimidation it conveyed.

Figure 8-3: The downward facing palm conveys dominance and control.

If you want to calm down a tense situation or ask for quiet, hold out both your palms slightly pointed downwards with your fingers slightly separated and gently beat them up and down. Make sure that your fingers are relaxed or you may just be fanning the flames of the fire!

Closed-palm, finger-pointed

Close your palm into a fist, point your index finger, and look out, world! You've just created a symbolic club for beating into submission anyone who's listening (see Figure 8-4).

Think back to a time when someone – a parent, teacher, or boss – pointed a finger at you and shook it for all it was worth. Don't be surprised if the memory makes you cringe. You know just how threatening and aggressive this gesture feels. That's because it comes from our primate ancestors who shake their 'fists' before pummelling their opposition into submission with a right over-arm blow. Ouch!

Figure 8-4: The closed-palm, pointed-finger is threatening and aggressive.

While you're remembering annoying gestures you'd rather forget, what about the one where the speaker beats her pointed finger in time to what she's saying. Again, it's as if you're being beaten with a sharp stick. It may make you feel like a naughty child being reprimanded.

The finger wag moves rhythmically sideways, back and forth like a metronome. Another annoying gesture, this action is a silent 'telling off' and reminds you of just how badly behaved you are.

The finger jab, the wag's closest cousin, is like a stabbing motion. Not one of the most conciliatory of gestures, use it at your peril.

If you habitually point and beat your finger when speaking, make a conscious effort to practise the palm-up and palm-down, fingers-loose positions. You find that you can create a positive impact on people and a relaxed atmosphere.

Hands Up!

Second only to your face, your hands are your most visually expressive feature and can be equated to your voice because they talk so much. They serve as a substitution for words as well as supporting the spoken word by illustrating and amplifying what you're saying. For example, when you're giving directions to someone who's lost, you most likely use your hands to get her back on the right path. When you're emphasising a point your hands move in time with your words. When you're describing a shape or a particular scene your hands create a visual picture of what you're saying. These kinds of hand gestures make complicated explanations more comprehensible.

Hiding your hands

When you conceal your hands by putting them behind your back or shoving them in your pockets, it's like keeping your mouth shut. What your hands are saying is, 'I don't want to talk!'

Take yourself back to your childhood. You've just been caught with your hand in the biscuit tin. You quickly pull it out and stick it behind your back while saying, 'No! Honestly! I didn't take anything!' And all the time your hand stays hidden.

Fast forward to your life now. You've been out on the town with your pals, you arrive home as the sun is rising, and your parent/spouse/partner asks you where you've been. Rather than owning up to whatever minor, or major, indiscretion you may have got into, if you're a man you most likely shove your hands into your pockets or cross your arms with your hands tucked neatly away while coming up with a good excuse. If you're a woman you busy your hands with a flurry of activities. Either way your palms stay hidden.

Many (many!) years ago when my husband Karl was starting off in sales he was told to watch the customers' hands when they were giving reasons why they couldn't buy his product. What he noticed was that when people were being honest with him they used their hands freely and often exposed their palms. He also noticed that when someone was being less than truthful her hand movements were reduced and kept more concealed.

The hand rub: Good for you or good for me?

When you rub your palms together you're signalling a positive expectation. How quickly you rub them indicates who's going to benefit. The slow palm rub can appear devious or crafty and may leave you feeling a little uneasy. You can bet that whatever positive result may happen is going to happen for anyone but you. The quick hand rub indicates excitement, pleasure, and enthusiasm. If someone is offering you an opportunity and is rubbing her hands together quickly as she speaks, you can feel assured that her proposal is good for you.

Consider these examples:

> ✔ A friend tells you how excited she is about a holiday she's about to take, a promotion she's been given, or a fabulous idea she's just had. She may well quickly rub her palms together with a big smile on her face.

> Once upon a time I lived and worked in Las Vegas, Nevada. No, I wasn't a showgirl! However, I occasionally went to the casinos and observed the gamblers. Something I noticed at the craps table was that people throwing the dice inevitably rubbed them together quickly before

throwing them. This action, along with the look on their faces, indicated that they were expecting something positive to happen. Most of the time something positive did happen, but for the casino, not the gambler.

✔ The car salesman or real estate agent sits you down and asks whether you're ready to pull out your cheque book, rubbing her hands slowly together as she does so. Meaning? Buyer beware!

✔ After taking all your relevant details about the purchase you want to make, the sales person rubs her palms together quickly and says, 'I've got just the thing for you!' Here the message is that she expects the results to be to *your* advantage. And if it works out for you, it probably works out for her. Everyone wins in this case!

The folded hand

You may think that folding your hands together is a positive gesture because it looks contained and controlled. But look again. Studies show that rather that demonstrating confidence, this gesture actually reveals frustration or hostility and signals that the person is holding a negative attitude. By folding your hands you're indicating that you're holding something in them that you don't want to let out.

Sure, some people may say that they're just comfortable with their hands folded in front of their waists, resting on a table, or in the fig leaf position protecting their private parts. And they may be. But because, like most gestures, this one is unconscious, you can be sure that more is going on than pure comfort.

The next time you're in a meeting and the speaker refuses to give anyone else a chance to talk, watch the hand positions of the rest of the group. They're likely to be in folded positions until someone finally interrupts, at which time the hands open as the person begins to speak.

If you're speaking with someone whose hands are clenched you can bet that she's holding annoyance, negativity, or frustration. Do whatever you can to get her to unlock her fingers to expose her palms. The longer they remain in the closed position the longer the hostile attitude remains.

Hands clenched

Think back to a time when you were really scared, nervous, or holding back a strong negative emotion. Chances are that you were clenching your hands for all you were worth and your knuckles were a bright white: the stronger the emotion, the tighter the clench. In addition to the strength of the clench you can also take meaning from where the clenched hands are placed.

In front of the face

Studies indicate that the higher the hands are held in the clenched position the stronger the negative mood (see Figure 8-5). So, if your boss is sitting with her elbows resting on her desk and her hands are clenched in front of her face, she's probably going to be difficult to handle. By putting her hands near her mouth she's indicating that she's holding back what she would like to say. Be careful not to push her too far. She just may unclench those hands and let the words fly out!

Figure 8-5: Hands in the clenched raised position indicate negativity.

Anne is a fast thinking, focused, and determined business-woman. She has numerous projects on the go at one time, all of which require her attention. She values her staff enormously and makes a point of having a few minutes of personal conversation with them all during the week. Most of them know that although she's genuinely interested in their wellbeing, she also likes people to get to the point and not go into too much detail. Nigel has worked for Anne for 16 years and likes to have a chat and a gossip. He frequently comes into Anne's office to do just that. The moment she sees him coming Anne puts her elbows on her desk and clenches her hands in front of her face. It's as though she's putting up a barrier to keep him from getting too close and to keep her from blurting out something she may later regret. Although Nigel doesn't seem to read the signals Anne's secretary knows that gesture is a sure sign of her frustration and annoyance. In order to shield Anne and protect Nigel's feelings she allows Nigel a few minutes of Anne's time before coming up with reasons why Anne has to end the conversation.

In the mid position

Say that you're working at your desk, frantically beavering away to meet a deadline, and someone comes in for a chat. Although you're quite annoyed about being interrupted you want to appear cordial and welcoming. You stop what you're doing, fold your hands on your desk in front of you, and ask, 'How may I help you?' Folding your hands and keeping them at this mid position signals that although you're irritated you're not yet ready to explode.

If the interloper is paying attention she sees that by holding your hands in a clenched position you're holding back a negative emotion. If she's smart she suggests coming back at a more convenient time.

The fig leaf

A lot of people stand with their hands folded in front of their private parts (see Figure 8-6). This position tells you that they're comfortable standing like that or that they don't know what to do with their hands. They're probably subconsciously feeling threatened and looking for a position that offers protection. By putting their hands in front of their most vulnerable parts they feel comfortable because they're covered. And, now their hands have something to do. Don't be fooled into thinking that this is a naturally confident position. The reason the position's comfortable is because it acts like a shield.

Figure 8-6: The fig leaf offers protection.

Letting the Fingers Do the Talking

If you look at the way people use their hands when they're speaking you can see that they often look like they're holding onto their words. These actions are based on the precision and power grips, which are the two ways you can hold onto an object.

Your hands and fingers also grab themselves when you're feeling under pressure, frustrated, or conversely, when you want to demonstrate control or authority. Even as I'm searching for the right way to convey this message I'm resting my elbows on my desk while I grip my palms in front of my face, watching the knuckles turn white. Finding no answer there I put my fingers to my mouth. Again, no luck. Shift to resting my chin in my palms as I search for inspiration. Even Henry, my dog, can tell by the way I'm using my hands that a struggle is going on here.

The precision grip

Hold something small between your thumb and fingertips. It can be a pen, a needle, or a delicate piece of fabric. This is the precision grip, shown in Figure 8-7, which allows you to hold and manipulate an object precisely.

Now, when you're speaking and want to say something accurately or delicately press your fingers and thumb together in a similar position with your palm facing towards you. Presto! Your listener understands that you're reinforcing what you're saying with great precision and accuracy.

Figure 8-7: The precision grip demonstrates exactness.

To focus your listener's attention and be seen as authoritative place your index finger against your thumb in the 'okay' gesture with your palm facing outward and your fingers softly rounded. This way you avoid intimidating your audience and you're likely to be perceived as thoughtful and goal oriented. This gesture is a favourite of modern politicians. Gosh, what a surprise!

In some countries the okay signal is considered rude. Before making any definite gesture find out what is acceptable behaviour and what may cause offence. (You can read more about the use of the okay signal in Chapter 12.)

When you ask a question or are feeling uncertain about a point you're making or responding to, you may well find that your thumb and index finger are almost – but not quite – touching (see Figure 8-8). Funny how that happens, as if the fingers know that the answer isn't quite there. When the fingers do come together in a definite grip it's as if they've grabbed the information and are holding onto it.

Figure 8-8: The thumb and forefinger not quite touching shows hesitancy or uncertainty.

The power grip

People who want to be perceived as strong, serious, and forceful use their whole fist to make a point (see Figure 8-9). It's as if they are holding onto a strap on a fast moving bus or hammering a nail into a block of wood.

You can use this gesture effectively in two ways. If you choose to deliver your message in a mild mannered way, leave your fingers bent, not fully closed. If, however, you mean business and are taking no prisoners, close your fingers into a fist and watch the fur fly.

Watch a public speaker or politician who deliberately wants to show just how much conviction and determination she has. Wow! Look at that tightly closed fist pumping up and down as if beating a big bass drum. Makes you wonder if more than a bit of showmanship is going on.

Figure 8-9: The power grip demonstrates conviction and determination.

Another similar gesture is the air punch, where you beat the air with a tightly closed fist to give force to a strong statement. This gesture is also the one you can use when your team scores, your proposal is accepted, or you win the lottery.

To show power but with a little less force than you would use in a tightly held power grip, let your fingers and thumb curl inwards as if they are loosely grasping an object. This is a way of getting people to take your message seriously without having to act out with an abundance of force.

If you're speaking to an audience and want to establish authority, let your fingers and thumb curve inwards as if they're almost but not quite holding an invisible object. You'll be perceived as in control and sure of what you're doing.

The power chop

Sometimes when you speak you may feel so passionate that you find yourself using your hand like a weapon, jabbing, punching, or chopping. Hopefully, you're just hitting empty air rather than a person or an object.

Your listener had better take you seriously when you use these gestures because they're a sure sign that whatever you're feeling is pretty strong and you aren't going to accept any arguments or contradictions. In other words, you mean business!

To demonstrate real forcefulness when you're speaking and to underline your determination to swash-buckle your way through the obstacle course, turn your hand into a symbolic axe blade by positioning it sideways with your fingers held closely together (see Figure 8-10). Now, make strong downward chopping movements. Your hand and arm start acting like a meat cleaver and woe betide the person who gets in your way.

The scissors or double-chop motion is a great one to use when you're rejecting or disagreeing with what someone else is saying. Cross both your forearms in front of your body and make outward cutting motions with your hands. You're indicating that you don't want to hear any more by cutting off the conversation.

Figure 8-10: The chopping gesture demonstrates clear conviction.

When my teenage son Max was doing his best to convince me why he should be allowed to travel the world on his own, I wasn't about to be swayed. His passionate arguments were countered with my motherly wisdom. Not only did my words say, 'No', everything I was doing was rejecting his proposal. It was when I combined the double-chop motion with the finger shake that my daughter Kristina came in with the conciliatory palms down, gently beating gesture that reduced the tension and created a modicum of calmness.

The steeple

In his studies of body movements, Ray Birdwhistell noted that confident, superior types of people whose gestures tend to be minimal or restricted 'steeple' their fingers to demonstrate their confident attitude. You can achieve this position by let-ting your finger tips lightly touch like the steeple on a building.

This gesture is also called the 'power position' because it's often used in a superior/subordinate interaction. Lawyers, accountants, and anyone in a position of authority frequently give instructions or advice with their fingers in this position.

✔ **The raised steeple:** When the fingers are raised in front of the chest, the speaker is giving thoughts or opinions.

Use the raised steeple position judiciously. Taken to extremes it can convey an arrogant 'know-it-all' attitude. If you tilt your head backwards when taking this position don't be surprised if you're perceived as smug or arrogant.

✔ **The lowered steeple:** When you're listening you may find your fingers in the lowered steeple position (see Figure 8-11). You look interested and ready to respond when you put your hands together like this. Women tend to use this position more often than the raised steeple.

Figure 8-11: The lowered steeple indicates a listening attitude.

Gripping hands, wrists, and arms

If you want to project superiority and confidence put your hands behind your back and grip one hand with the other. Look at prominent male members of royal families around the world. Observe senior military personnel, police officers patrolling their beats, or the headmaster of your local school striding through the corridors. They all adopt this position of authority. They are showing no fear of exposing their vulnerable necks, hearts, or stomachs to potential threats and hazards.

The next time you're in a stressful or uncomfortable situation, adopt the palm-in-palm-behind-the-back stance. Note how your feelings change from frustrated, insecure, or angry to relaxed and confident.

As the grip moves up the arm, though, the meaning changes. You can bet that if someone is gripping her wrist behind her back rather than just her hand she's holding back frustration. This gesture is a way of maintaining self-control, as if the hand is holding the wrist or arm to keep it from hitting out. The farther up the back the hand goes the greater the level of frustration. By the time the hand reaches the upper arm this person may have moved from frustration to anger. This gesture is also a sign of nervousness and is an attempt at self-control.

Gesturing with your thumbs

Gestures associated with the thumb convey dominance, superiority, and in some cases aggression so it's not surprising that in palmistry the thumb denotes strength of character and ego. If you've ever heard the expression 'under the thumb' you know the implication is that the person with the thumb is the one in control. Woe betide the person under the thumb, as according to ancient Roman history the thumb turned down served as a sign of imminent death.

✔ **Thumbs up:** The thumb up position generally denotes agreement. But be careful using this gesture as in some cultures it's perceived as rude and highly offensive.

- **Thumbs protruding from a person's pockets:** This gesture demonstrates dominance and self-assuredness. Although both men and women use this gesture, it's the rare woman who adopts the position of holding her jacket lapel with the thumb exposed, whereas men often do.

- **Gesturing towards another person with your thumb:** When you use your thumb to point towards someone else, you're being dismissive, disrespectful, or ridiculing the other person.

Andrew had the unfortunate habit of ridiculing Jane, his wife, in front of their friends. When they were in company he would often refer to her as 'the little woman' gesturing in her direction with a closed fist, using his thumb as a pointer. Although Jane told him how irritating she found this gesture, as well as the accompanying remarks, Andrew took no notice. He did notice, however, when after several years of rude and disrespectful behaviour Jane divorced him.

Analysing Handshakes

Shaking hands upon meeting is a tradition that creates a bond of solidarity. Our ancestors in their caves greeted one another with out-stretched arms and exposed palms to show they were free of clubs and other life-threatening weapons. Scuttle along to the Roman period, where it was common to carry concealed daggers up ones sleeve. Hence, two men would grab each other's lower arms as a means of greeting and to check out the other's intentions.

As the handshake evolved it became a gesture to cement agreements, offer a welcome, and bid someone farewell. Therefore, make sure that when you shake hands the gesture is open, congenial, and positive.

Deciding who reaches out first

Although shaking hands when meeting another person for the first time is customary, in some instances making the first move may not be appropriate. For example, if you've forced the meeting or the other person is uncomfortable in your presence it would be inappropriate for you to extend your hand as a sign of trust and welcome. Yet if you consider the person you're meeting to be your equal and you're both glad to see one another, you simultaneously extend your hands in greeting.

When you show up at a customer's without having been invited wait to see if she extends her hand in welcome. If you put your hand out first she may feel forced to shake your hand, creating a negative feeling. If no handshake is forthcoming, give a small nod of your head instead.

Because some people aren't sure whether or not to shake a woman's hand in a business context, the woman should extend her hand first to show that she's comfortable to shake hands. That way avoids wondering and fumbling.

Conveying attitude

Some people shake hands as if they're Attila the Hun about to put you in your place. Others remain passive and detached, barely offering you a fingertip. Still others present you with a cold, clammy hand reminiscent of a wet mackerel. How people shake hands tells you a lot about them, their attitude, and their feelings about the person they're about to touch.

University of Alabama professor William Chaplin and his students examined the relationship between personality and styles of handshakes. They found that extroverted and emotionally expressive people are inclined to shake hands firmly whereas neurotic and shy people don't. They also found that women who have an open attitude to new experiences use a firm handshake.

The bone cruncher

Before you can stuff your hand in your pocket the Bone Cruncher is there, turning your knuckles into pulverised bone. These people seem to have an overly aggressive attitude to compensate for their ineffectualness. The Bone Cruncher is to be avoided when it comes to shaking hands because you can do little to counter the action.

To avoid a potentially painful handshake both men and women should avoid wearing rings on your right hands in a business context.

If you think that your hand has been purposely crunched say 'Wow! That's one strong grip and it really hurt!' You're letting the person know that you're onto her game. This has even more impact if other people are present observing the interaction. She's unlikely to play that trick again.

George lacks social skills and is unaware of how much pressure he puts into his handshakes. He unconsciously makes up for his social ineptness by putting an extra hard squeeze into his grasp. Women find it especially uncomfortable to shake hands with George. He squeezes their hands so forcefully that it's not uncommon for women to walk away from having shaken hands with George sporting red welts where their rings have cut into their fingers. One friend mused, 'If he does that shaking hands I wonder what happens when he kisses you?'

The wet fish

If you've ever been presented with a totally limp hand to shake you know how unconnected it feels when your hands meet. People who refuse to commit to a handshake tend to be self-important and aloof. Granted, surgeons and concert pianists need to guard their fingers and are known for their soft handshakes. And people who have to do a lot of shaking also offer a relaxed hand in order to protect their fingers.

Some people offer the uncommitted handshake for other reasons. Some women think that it's appealing to present themselves as submissive to both men and women. Very strong people sometimes offer a soft handshake as a way of highlighting their physical power. If a person's lacking in confidence she also holds back from making a connection.

Bonnie comes from Dallas, Texas, and works for a large investment firm in London. Her working environment is predominantly male. Although she's highly accomplished, her boss and peers perceive her as being quite submissive. One of the reasons for this is because of the way she shakes hands. Regardless of the million pound deals she regularly lands, she still highlights her femininity by offering a soft handshake, as she was taught to do growing up in the southern USA.

Although in a social context this approach may appeal to men, in the business environment her male colleagues regularly joke about the Southern Belle and her wily ways.

The power shake

At times you may want to show that you have the upper hand, meaning that you're strong and in control. You can do this by making sure that your hand faces down in the handshake. Although your palm doesn't have to be completely turned over so that it faces directly downward, the slight turning shows that you're in charge.

Even if you unconsciously place your hand in the top position you have the automatic advantage. This is because the hand down position is associated with dominance and control whereas the upward facing palm conveys compliance and passivity. Even if you and the receiver are unaware of your hand positions, you feel more dominant and the other person feels more submissive.

The double-hander

The double-hander is a favourite in the corporate and political arena. Through this particular handshake, the initiator aims to portray sincerity, honesty, and a deep feeling for the receiver. By using it you increase the amount of physical contact and by restricting the receiver's right hand you gain control of the interaction. Because the double-hander is like a mini hug choose your receiver carefully. Ideally, this handshake should only be used where a personal relationship already exists.

If someone thrusts her hand towards you, palm facing downwards, and grabs your hand in hers putting you in a submissive position with little chance of balancing the equation, what do you do? Allow the power player to take your hand with your palm facing upwards. Then, before she knows what you're up to, put your left hand on top of her right to create a double-hander. From this position you're able to straighten the handshake and gain control subtly and effectively.

When you use the two-handed handshake, the left hand conveys two points worth noting. Firstly, it reveals the intensity of feeling you're demonstrating towards the receiver. The higher up the arm your left hand goes, as shown in Figure 8-12, the deeper the level of intimacy you want to show. This is a complex movement in that the gesture shows both the degree of connection you have with the receiver as well as the amount of control you're exerting. The second point is that your left hand invades the receiver's personal space. Unless the receiver has positive feelings for you this gesture can lead to feelings of suspicion and mistrust. If in doubt, don't use it; especially on your boss.

The leach

Some people just don't know when to let go. They grab your hand, shake it, and then hang on until you want to pry their fingers off. This is a subtle way of demonstrating control. By prolonging the contact they're engaging you for longer than you may have wanted. Interestingly, you'll probably allow the contact to remain until you can think of a good reason to pull away. Such as, 'Excuse me, I have to go now' even though you may have just arrived!

Figure 8-12: Intimacy and control increase as the left hand moves up the arm.

The space invader

Whether you're pulling someone into your territory when shaking hands or you're invading her space by plunging your arm into her terrain, a power play is taking place and you hold the power (see Figure 8-13).

In the first instance, you propel your arm forward, forcefully grip the receiver's extended hand, and simultaneously go into a quick reverse thrust, yanking her into your space and huddling over the handshake until you're ready to let it go. If you pull someone into your personal space you create a hand-shake on your terms. You're in charge.

Be aware of the amount of force you apply or you may find the other person falling on top of you as you pull her in. That's what you call getting the relationship off on the wrong foot!

Figure 8-13: Space invaders demand power and control.

If you invade the other person's territory you extend your arm fully, forcing the other person to retreat back into her domain. Her arm ends up in a cramped position while your extended arm fills her space.

The firm shake

If you want to create a sense of mutual respect and equality make sure that when you shake hands with another person both your palms are in the vertical position, your fingers are wrapped around one another's hands, and that you apply the same amount of pressure. Your hands should meet in no-man's land, halfway between your space and the other person's.

Taking the left side advantage

The next time you look at a photograph of two leaders standing next to one another see if one looks more dominant than the other. Chances are that you perceive the person on the left side of the picture to have the edge.

If the photograph shows them shaking hands you can easily see that the hand of the person on the left is in the upper position, making her appear more powerful and in control. Savvy politicians are aware of the impact this body position makes and jockey to place themselves to the right of their colleague, or adversary, in order to come out on the left in the photo.

To gain the left side advantage to make yourself appear as if you're calling the shots, position yourself to the right of the other person. If you want to increase your power play, place your left hand on your colleague's back while shaking hands. Although the other person may feel annoyed by your obvious power play, you can smile warmly, knowing that you've got the advantage.

Displacing Your Energy

If you ever noticed yourself drumming your fingers, pulling your earlobe, touching your face, or scratching your head when you haven't got an itch, you're experiencing displacement activities. Displacement activities are easy to spot because they are the small, inconsequential gestures you make when you're feeling inner turmoil or frustration.

People who are experiencing frustration or internal conflict often feel the need to take action. If they struggle to find an appropriate action to address the source of annoyance they fill the void with meaningless activities to keep themselves busy.

Drumming for relief

If you're in a meeting and someone's drumming her fingers on the table, pay attention. This person is telling you something. Bored, frustrated, or even irritated; the percussionist is impatient.

Stephen works for an international law firm. He recently found out that his colleagues call him 'Thumper' because of his constant finger drumming during meetings. Stephen reveals his state of mind by the tempo of his finger tapping. When he's bored he drums the four fingers of his right hand in quick succession. When he's thoughtfully considering a suggestion he quietly taps his middle finger. When he's prepared to conclude the meeting he knocks his knuckles on the table. Without saying a word his colleagues know what Stephen's thinking.

Fiddling for comfort

Notice what you do the next time you feel anxious. Chances are you'll fiddle with an object. You may jangle your keys, twist a ring on your finger, or adjust your clothes. You may also touch yourself by picking at your nails, tugging your earlobe, rubbing your cheek, or running your fingers through your hair. The purpose of these actions is to ease any nervousness you may be feeling.

When people are feeling anxious they focus their excess energy onto themselves as a way of providing temporary relief. These actions are sometimes referred to as 'adaptors' because they help you adapt to your internal tension. Adaptive behaviours are mainly focused on the head and the face. Unconsciously you may find yourself stroking your face, running your fingers over your lips, or rubbing the back of your neck when you're feeling upset. These hand gestures are reminiscent of those your mother may have used to comfort you when you were a child.

Hand to nose

When your hand goes to your nose you know a falsehood is going on inside. Whether you're telling a deliberate lie (as if), having a dishonest thought, pretending to be brave when you're totally terrified, or simply feeling a moment of self-doubt, the hand going to your nose is the signal.

As I was walking my dog Henry, thinking about my day's challenges, I began to notice that each time I moved from one thought to the next my hand made a definite movement. I particularly noticed when I wiped my nose, a sign of falsehood and doubt. Granted, it was cold, my body was warm, and my nose was running, so I had to wipe it. But at the time I had been thinking that I'd be able to meet a deadline when, in fact, I seriously doubted that I would.

The act of self-touching signals a need for reassurance. Rubbing the nose, giving it a quick wipe, or a simple scratch are responses to the tingling sensation caused by heightened blood flow to the nose when you're feeling stressed.

To tell if someone's feeling under pressure, observe her hand to face gestures.

Hand to cheek

The hand to cheek gesture indicates boredom, uninterest, and fatigue. Resting your hand on your cheek is like resting your hand on your pillow. Before you know it you may be nodding off into dreamland. In meetings, lectures, and restaurants you see people resting their heads on their hands as negative feelings creep in.

If you're speaking in a public forum and you notice heads are resting in hands, change what you're doing. The change catches their attention and saves you the embarrassment of heads collapsing into hands in an embarrassing heap.

Hand to chin

The chin resting on the top of the hand is a sign of thinking: The person's pondering something. The thumb under the chin with the index finger pointing up the side of the face signals that an evaluation is being made. She's listened and now she's making an assessment.

Recent photographs of Hillary Rodham Clinton show her posing in the evaluation posture, with her chin resting on her thumb and her index finger pointing up her chin. The pose indicates that she's weighing up the merits of the argument.

Chapter 9

Standing Your Ground

● ●

In This Chapter

▶ Finding the right stance for your attitude

▶ Showing how you really feel

▶ Revealing information without meaning to

● ●

*A*t certain times in your life you've had to take a stance
and make a firm decision. You probably planted your
feet firmly on the ground and got on with what you had to do.
At other times you've been able to take it easy, wandering
from one pillar to another post.

You've stamped your foot in anger – or known someone who
has – you've rubbed your ankle up against another's as well
as your own, and you've stood with your weight on one leg in
boredom, as well as bouncing on your toes in excitement.

In this chapter I look at the different types of stance you adopt
depending on your mood and circumstances. You also discover
what the swinging foot is saying, as well as the pointed toe.

Showing Commitment and Attitude through Your Stance

The foundation for any stance is to stand with your feet
evenly placed under your hips and with your weight equally
distributed between them. What you choose to do with that
foundation depends on what you want to show and how you
want to be perceived. How you hold yourself reflects the
effects of life experiences as well as social position.

You can spot status by the way a person stands. The Queen doesn't slump, at least, not in public. The petty officer stands to attention when his superior enters the room. The servant bows at his master's will.

The person who slouches, who lets his head droop, his shoulders hunch, and his feet turn inwards shows submission, a lack of commitment, and indicates that he's withdrawing, or holding back. Conversely, people who place their weight evenly between their legs, with their feet firmly planted under them, look confident and self-assured, providing the other body parts are working in harmony with the feet and legs. When standing in this position the natural inclination is to hold your head high, shoulders back, and stomach in. Presto! You're standing like a winner.

If you want to assess a person's attitude, look at how he's standing. Most people make the majority of their important decisions when both of their feet are on the ground. If you want to be perceived as powerful, influential, and in control, stand with your legs slightly apart with your weight evenly distributed between them.

Straddle stance

The straddle stance is a stable position and the one most favoured by those who are showing dominance. It requires that your legs are straight, and that your feet are placed wide apart with your weight equally distributed between them.

With their higher centre of gravity, men adopt the straddle stance more frequently than women. Their height notwithstanding, men also adopt this position more frequently in the company of other people when they're using their posture as a means of communication.

The expressions 'Having your feet on the ground' and 'Standing on your own two feet' refer to the ancient Chinese custom of binding women's feet. This custom was mostly reserved for royalty and meant that the women whose feet had been bound were unable to stand on their own two feet without causing pain.

Macho messages

A resolutely immovable posture, in which someone has planted his feet so firmly that there's no room for budging, tells you that he's standing his ground (see Figure 9-1). He's also showing you who's boss by filling more space and covertly presenting his bits.

During his last year at junior school, Tommy, aged twelve, was in the school's winning rugby team. At the celebration party after the match, a group of boys stood in a circle, talking amongst themselves. As proud winners, each one of them had adopted the straddle stance, demonstrating his commonality and team spirit. Even at such a young age the boys were showing their machismo and their solidarity.

Figure 9-1: The straddle stance strongly conveys messages of dominance and power.

If you're feeling defeated and want to change your mood, adopt the straddle stance, with your head held high, and your shoulders back. By adopting this powerful position, you can create the matching feeling.

Threatening signs

Throughout history and across cultures, phallic displays have been considered signs of dominance. By standing with his legs apart, a man unashamedly shows his crotch to anyone who's looking, declaring himself to be Conan the Warrior. Exposing himself this way, even though he may be fully covered, demonstrates that as far as he's concerned, he's the boss.

You can tell if two people are ready to fight, or are merely summing up each other in a friendly way. If they stand face to face with their feet apart, their hands on their hips, or their fingers and thumbs tucked into their belt loops or the tops of their pockets, they probably don't like one another very much and are looking for trouble. If, however, their bodies are turned slightly away from one another they're simply sizing each other up in a friendly interchange.

A dominant male baboon exposes and flaunts his erect penis as a signal to the other male baboons of his power and position. Men in New Guinea proclaim their position in the community by the size and decorative features of their penis sheaths. European males in the 15th and 16th centuries wore codpieces as a sign of virility and status.

In the latest James Bond film the British actor, Daniel Craig, strides out of the ocean wearing a swimsuit that unashamedly draws the eye to his crotch. The light blue colour of the swimwear, combined with Craig's well-endowed and highly toned body, highlights the character's strength and power.

Parallel stance

The parallel stance (shown in Figure 9-2) is a subordinate position where the legs are straight and the feet are placed closely together. It's a position taken if you are called up in front of the headmaster, reporting to your commanding officer, or standing in front of a judge, awaiting sentence.

Figure 9-2: The parallel stance is a sign of uncertainty and submission.

Feet placed closely together reduce the foundation for standing and make the stance more precarious. You can easily push someone over from this position if you were to catch him off guard. People who aren't sure about their position on a subject adopt the parallel stance. Standing with their legs closely placed together they're indicating that they feel hesitant or tentative. A wider stance provides a broader and firmer foundation. It is much harder to unbalance a person who's standing with his legs separated (refer to the preceding section 'Straddle stance').

When Max received his school's Naval Cadet of the Year Award he had to march across the quad, outfitted in full dress uniform. His stride was firm and his legs moved crisply. His shoulders were back and upright. When he reached his commanding officer he smartly placed his feet together and kept his position held high. By standing to attention, with his legs straight and his feet closely placed together, in front of his commanding officer, he was demonstrating both his respect and his subservience.

Taking a stance

To experience the contrasting sensations, attitudes, and impressions that result from standing in the straddle and parallel positions do the following exercise.

This exercise requires a full length mirror.

1. Stand in front of the mirror.

2. Observe how you are standing.

3. Adopt the parallel stance.

4. Hold this position for fifteen seconds.

5. Observe yourself closely and identify the feelings you experience from standing in this position.

What feelings, thoughts, or attitudes did you experience standing in that position? What image does that posture convey to you? How does your response to that image affect your self-perception?

Repeat this exercise, this time standing in the straddle stance. Ask yourself the same questions as in the previous exercise. What differences do you notice?

Buttress stance

Built against or projecting from a wall, buttresses are architectural structures designed to support or reinforce the wall to which they are attached. In a more general sense, the word suggests support, as in one person buttressing another person's arguments.

In the buttress stance you place most of your weight on a straight supporting leg, allowing your other leg to serve as a buttress. This non-weightbearing leg can be straight or bent. Whichever it is, the foot most likely points away from where the rest of the body is facing.

Although people adopting the buttress stance say they're just resting comfortably, this position signals that the person wants to get away. The stance bears a close resemblance to the act of walking. Just before moving, you shift your weight to one leg in order that the other is free to take a step. Although you may not choose to move from the buttress stance, your legs are positioned so that they easily can. This position gives a cleverly disguised message, saying that you want to go.

If you see someone repeatedly shifting his weight from one foot to the other while in conversation with you, he's signalling that he's ready to take leave of your company.

If you notice someone standing with one leg serving as a buttress, take a look at the direction in which the toe of his buttress foot is pointing. The direction the foot takes frequently points to the object the person is thinking about. It may be pointed in the direction of someone who's caught his eye, but it most often points in the direction of his escape route.

Scissor stance

Think of your legs as if they were the two blades of a pair of scissors. Cross one over the other, keeping your knees straight, and you're in the classic scissors stance. This is an obvious defensive gesture, because the person is doing his best to protect his most precious parts without resorting to putting his hands over his jewels. (For physiological reasons it's easier for women to adopt the tightly closed scissors position than it is for men.)

When one leg is crossed over the other and one of the two knees is bent, the position is called the 'bent blade stance'. Someone standing in the scissors stance or the bent blade stance is demonstrating his immobility. The feet are placed in such a way that a speedy departure is impossible without legs and feet struggling to uncoil themselves.

Crossed legs, especially in the standing position, relay varying messages:

- ✓ **Negativity, defensiveness, and insecurity:** Crossing your legs is a defensive position. The gesture often accompanies the crossed arm position, reinforcing the barrier. If legs only are crossed, the suggestion of defensive or negative feelings is less strong than crossed arms.

- ✓ **Commitment and immobility:** A person standing with his legs crossed when in conversation is showing that he's committed to the interaction and has no intention of leaving.

- ✓ **Submission:** The crossed leg position comes across as submissive because the stance conveys no sign of impatience.

If someone tells you that he's standing with his legs and arms crossed because he's cold, see how his hands and legs are positioned. Someone who's really cold tucks his hands into his armpits, or hugs himself. His legs are stiff, straight, and pushed tightly against each other.

In a gathering of people, those who don't know one another well tend to stand slightly apart from each other, with their arms and legs in a crossed position. Their jackets are likely to be buttoned as well, giving a complete picture of people who are feeling submissive or defensive because they are symbolically denying access to themselves.

Entwining your legs

Some gestures are particular to men and others are particular to women. The leg twine in which the top of one foot locks itself around the other leg is used almost exclusively by women. This position highlights insecurity and resembles a tortoise in retreat.

If you want to unlock a woman from the entwined leg position take a friendly and low-key approach to her in order to get her to open up.

Fran was asked by her History of Art university lecturer to stand in front of the lecture hall and discuss the latest assignment. Being uncertain of what was expected of her, she stood in front of the class of 120 students, with one foot drawn up behind her supporting leg and pressed against her calf. Although she was confident about her knowledge of the material, she felt shy and timid speaking in front of such a large group of people, many of whom she didn't know. When she realised how she was standing, she placed both feet firmly under her and found that she felt more confident and secure, and was able to speak with authority and assurance.

Research shows that the body reflects the mind's state. Studies show that people meeting in a group for the first time usually stand with their arms and legs in the crossed position. As rapport develops and they become more comfortable with one another they release the closed pose, and open up their bodies. The procedure follows a predictable pattern that entails uncrossing their legs first and placing their feet in the parallel pose. The arms and hands unfold, and become animate. When the people feel comfortable and at ease they move from the parallel stance to an open position in which the feet are slightly apart and facing the other person. Similarly, indicators of someone who has withdrawn from the conversation are crossed arms and legs. A person sitting in this position is unlikely to be convinced by anything you may say or do.

Reflecting Your Feelings by the Way You Position Your Feet

Because your feet are the farthest point from your brain, your grey matter has less control over them than it does, say, over your hands or facial expressions. You're less aware of where your feet are facing and what they're doing than you are of your eyes, which are about as close to your brain as they can get.

Pointing towards the desired place

Humans evolved with two legs, the purpose of which is to move forward towards what you want and move away from what you don't want. The direction in which your feet point tells the observer where you want to go. We've all experienced talking to someone you know who would rather be anyplace else than with you. While his face is smiling and his head nodding, his feet are pointing away from you (see Figure 9-3).

When the feet, head, and torso are pointing in the same direction you're showing an open, or dominant, attitude.

d is going. Like a magnet, they point in the direction of someone who appeals to you.

Ros is a vivacious, attractive woman who men flock to. At a recent party she was flanked by a group of three men who struggled to take their eyes off her. Each man stood with his front foot pointed toward her, silently indicating his interest. Her feet shifted from man to man, reeling each of them in like a fish on the line until she shifted her foot position towards her next target. All the time, her face was smiling and her body was in an open position, demonstrating her ingenuousness and warmth.

Figure 9-3: The woman is indicating that she'd like to leave, while the man wants to hold her attention.

Your feet act as pointers, signalling where your min

If you want to show someone that you find him attractive, point your foot in his direction. When you're interested in a particular conversation, or another person, place one foot forward towards the person, shortening the distance between the two of you. If you're not interested in the person, or in what he's saying, keep your feet back. If you're seated, and are speaking with another person who holds no interest for you, pull your feet back under your chair.

If you're in conversation with another person and notice that he doesn't seem entirely engaged with you, look at where his feet are pointing.

Wolfgang and Daniela were at a party. It was late and Wolfie was tired, bored, and wanted to be in his own bed watching television. While he and Daniela were saying their good-byes, Wolfie couldn't understand why he was having so much difficulty in getting Daniela to leave. Had Wolfie looked, he would have seen that while they were saying goodbye to their host, Daniela's feet remained pointed in the host's direction, whereas Wolfie's feet were heading towards the door.

Fidgeting feet

Fidgeting feet are a good indicator of someone's impatience threshold. The feet say they want to flee and so are forced to fidget until the time comes to walk or run. If you're standing, you may repeatedly tap your foot to indicate your impatience. If you're sitting with your legs crossed, you may twitch the hanging foot up and down, or back and forth.

To appear calm on the outside when everything inside's in a panic, breathe from your abdomen, adjust your stance, and let your feet take root.

Knotted ankles

Whether you're sitting or standing, if you've knotted or twisted your ankles together, the sign you're giving is that you're locked in and not budging. Locked ankles reflect a closed, insecure, or a negative attitude, suggesting ambiguity, or revealing a lack of confidence. Knotted ankles are definitely not a sign of someone who's feeling confident and in command.

People who say they're comfortable sitting with their ankles tightly crossed probably are. Their bodies are reflecting their mental state, and there's no tension between the two. Whether they confess that they're comfortable because their actions are reflecting their attitude – which according to the signs may be nervous, anxious, or defensive – depends on how comfortable they are in admitting their emotional state.

To appear more open, confident, and approachable, uncross your ankles.

When Shaun first began running training sessions he was quite nervous standing in front of a large group, many of whom he didn't know personally. When he watched himself on videotape he discovered that he was standing with his ankles crossed in front of him. As he moved across the stage, like a figure skater, he would push off with one foot, crossing one leg behind, or in front of, the other. As a result of seeing himself in action, Shaun was able to adjust his behaviour. Now when he walks across the stage he moves with purpose, placing one foot in front of the other.

Observe the differences in how men and women sit in the crossed ankle position. Men often clench their fists, resting them on their knees, or tightly grip the arms of the chair. Their legs are splayed, exposing their open crotch. Women tend to hold their knees together, with their feet often placed to one side, their hands resting in their laps side by side, or with one placed on top of the other.

The Army expression 'keeping your heels locked' means that, if a matter is not your personal concern, you aren't to disclose what you don't have to.

Twitching, flicking, or going in circles

If you suspect someone of lying to you, or holding back information, look at his feet. Research on deception reveals that a person who's asked to lie shows more signs of fraud below the waist than above. Are his feet twitching, flicking, or going around in circles?

Hand and eye movements are under conscious control. Because they are close to your brain and a main source of communication, you're more aware of what they're doing than you are of your legs and feet which, no matter how short you are, are still quite far from your brain.

Leaking information isn't restricted to deception. For example, people showing interest in another person use their bodies to reveal what their minds are thinking and their mouths mustn't tell. Say that a man is speaking to a woman he finds particularly attractive. He's very likely to stand with one foot pointing toward her with his legs apart exposing his groin area, and holding his arms in a splayed position to make himself look larger and fill more space. If the woman doesn't find him attractive and wants to give him the brush-off, she holds her legs together, faces her body away from him, folds her arms, and makes herself appear as small as possible. No one says a word, yet the visual messages tell the story (see Figure 9-4).

Figure 9-4: Although the man may be coming on strong, the woman's not committing.

Walking Styles

Some people slump and drag their feet. Others add a lively bounce to their step. Still others swagger, shuffle, or career along a path. However a person walks, he's being true to his internal rhythms, feelings, and emotions. Or, he's presenting an image of what he wants you to believe. Watching people walk can tell you a lot about their health, attitude, and general state of being.

How you walk reflects your mental state. Vivacious, healthy, and energetic people walk faster than people who are elderly, ill, or infirm. The energetic walker swings his arms high, both in front and behind, sometimes giving the appearance of marching. For the most part, young people have more muscle flexibility than older people and can move faster, giving the appearance of energy and excitement.

If you find yourself feeling depressed and dragging your feet as you walk along, increase your tempo. A quicker pace increases your energy and lifts your spirits.

The exaggerated walking style adopted by military personnel deliberately conveys the image of dynamism and forceful vitality.

Part IV

Putting the Body Into Social and Business Context

The 5th Wave   By Rich Tennant

"When we met, we seemed to be on the same track, so we hitched up. Then, just when I thought the relationship was gaining steam, something derailed it. I don't know. Maybe I was sending the wrong signals."

In this part . . .

In this part I take you on a trip from the office, to the bar, then overseas to experience different countries and cultures. In the boardroom you find out where to place and position yourself for greatest effect. In the dating arena you discover how to read and reveal signs of interest and dismissal and how to engage with a possible romantic partner. In sampling different cultures I warn you of body language pitfalls to avoid, and tips to utilise to improve your relationships with people from all over the world.

Chapter 10

Territorial Rights and Regulations

● ●

In This Chapter

▶ Fitting into your space

▶ Staking your claim

▶ Positioning yourself to your best advantage

● ●

*1*f you've ever bumped into a stranger on the high street, if you've ever been squashed on a rush hour tube, or if you've ever been kissed by someone you'd rather hadn't kissed you, you've experienced space invasion. Unless invited, it feels a bit creepy when someone gets too close. And it feels, oh so good, when the distance's right.

In this chapter you look at the different areas of space around you. You find out why what feels comfortable at ten paces feels differently at one. You also discover why cohorts sit side by side and adversaries sit face to face. Finally, you discover how the way that you position yourself, whether upright, supine, or simply off kilter, impacts on your gestures, movements, and the impression you make.

Understanding the Effect of Space

The way you fill and move within space impacts your attitude, your feelings, and the way that others perceive you. People who know where to position themselves in relation to someone else control the interaction. They know when to get up close and personal, and when to back off. They know the different implications between standing so close to another person that you can feel that person's breath, and standing so far away that you have to squint to see one another. By knowing where and how to place yourself in relation to another person, you can consciously control that person's perception of you.

Territorial parameters aren't just a matter of manners. Foreign invaders, rival gangs, trespassers, burglars, pushy bullies, and aggressive drivers all know that their invasion into another's territory can be met with varying degrees of resistance. Zoologist Desmond Morris sees humans as competitive as well as cooperative creatures. As humans strive for dominance, systems must be put in place to avoid chaos. Territorial perimeters, where everyone knows and respects one another's space, is one cooperative system.

A man is said to be king of his castle. As reigning sovereign, whether your castle is a flat in the heart of the city, a country farmhouse, or a caravan, you know that you've the right to be dominant in your own territory. And, everyone else has the right to be dominant in his. When someone enters your space without being invited, you may feel a little edgy. Whether it's fighter planes attacking from above, or a mother bursting into her teenage son's room, the likelihood is that the person whose space has been invaded is going to fight back.

Although you may feel perfectly confident, comfortable, and at home in one surrounding, when you enter another, your feelings change. Say that you work in your own office. You feel comfortable and in control of your environment because you're in familiar surroundings. Then you're called into your boss's office. Suddenly the comfort level changes. You're now entering someone else's territory and the control shifts from you to the person whose space you've penetrated. Your body language changes from dominant to submissive without you even realising it.

Knowing Your Space

Humans have circles of space around them, which range from no space at all (touching) to far enough away that, even though you can be seen, you're not close enough to touch.

As with animals, humans protect their territory by following accepted codes of behaviour. Whereas birds sing to proclaim their dominance over a particular part of a hedgerow, and dogs lift their legs to stake claim to a lamppost, humans indicate through their body movements what they perceive to be their territory, and how near and how far a person may penetrate it.

The five zones

In his book, *The Hidden Dimension*, the American anthropologist Edward T Hall, defined *proxemics* as the study of the human use of space within the context of culture. Understanding that cultural influences impact upon how people move within their space, and the amount of space a person is comfortable with, Hall divided space into five distinct areas. The relationship you have with another person determines how near you allow that person to come to you.

Hall defined five concentric spatial zones that affect behaviour:

- **Close Intimate (0–15 centimetres/0–6 inches):** This space is saved for lovers, close friends and family members. It's a position for the most intimate behaviours, including touching, embracing, and kissing.

- **Intimate (15–45 centimetres/6–18 inches):** This space is where the lover, friend, and relatives are welcome. The distance is comfortable and secure. You feel uncomfortable, and your body reacts protectively, if a stranger, someone you don't know well, or someone you don't like, enters this space.

- **Personal (45 centimetres–1.2 metres/18 inches–4 feet):** For most Westerners, this distance is the most comfortable for personal conversations. If you step too far into the space, the other person may feel threatened. If you stand outside of the space, the other person can feel rebuffed.

- **Social (1.2–3.6 metres/4–12 feet):** When you're in a business-based interaction with shop assistants and tradespeople, this area is where you feel most comfortable. If you stand within the inner parameter, you're perceived as being too familiar. If you stand outside the outer ring, you're perceived as rude and stand-offish.

> ✔ **Public (3.6 metres +/12 feet +):** If you're speaking to an audience in a formal setting, the distance between yourself and the first row is in the public space. Any closer and you feel intruded upon; your communication feels cramped. Any farther away and you feel distanced from your listener, making it harder to connect with them.

The distance people keep between themselves reveals their relationship and how they feel about the other person.

Other territorial positions

In addition to your space bubble's five concentric circles, you have another set of territorial positions, private and personal to you. You have:

> ✔ **Inner space:** Your internal thoughts and feelings.
>
> ✔ **Immediate outer space:** Friends, family, close colleagues.
>
> ✔ **Your public arena:** The larger world in which you interact with an assortment of people.

People who enjoy their own company and prefer to keep to themselves have few requirements. They live quieter, simpler lives than those who surround themselves with people and fill their lives with social activities.

People who live lives that involve lavish entertaining need space to accommodate all the individuals and the accompanying accessories that go with a socially active life. Their personalities require a broad expanse of space.

A person who has many people taking up much of his time occasionally draws into his inner space for quiet contemplation. Executives, politicians, busy parents, and professionals – as well as the ubiquitous celebrity – need time alone to recharge their batteries.

Big personalities fill their space with their movements. For example, they hold their arms farther from their bodies than people with quieter personalities. Their gestures are definite and they move with purpose. People whose personalities are more internally directed use fewer and smaller gestures.

Space also works in proportion to status. Presidents, senior partners, and chief executives require a copious amount of resources, including space, in a practical sense and to fill status expectations, both their own and others.

Pauline is a Human Resources (HR) specialist, working in the telecoms industry. When she was promoted to the role of HR director, she moved from her open plan office to a private office of her own. Although the room wasn't large, it had windows and a door to close herself off. Knowing that she needed thinking time as well as time for interacting with her team, Pauline appreciated the way that she was able to manage her public and private space according to the requirements.

Growing up in Palm Beach, Florida, a town of great opulence and wealth, I often saw 12-bedroom mansions for a family of four. The size of people's homes reflected their status – large homes indicated large incomes and large personalities. Small homes indicated lower income and lower status. My mother's home in Palm Beach had two bedrooms that cosily accommodated my mother, my sister, and myself. Mom was a single mother, struggling to raise her two daughters. She didn't entertain much and had little use for a lot of space. Half a mile away was the winter home of the late President John F Kennedy. His home was huge in comparison, with high walls surrounding the property and bodyguards walking the grounds. The President's position of power, status, and authority came with more needs than that of a young divorcee on a restricted budget.

You can tell a person's status by how much personal space he requires. The more space expected and offered, the higher the status.

How you view and define your space determines how others respond. By being clear about how far a person may come into your territory, you make it easier for others to know your boundaries and behave accordingly.

Using Space

Whether you're protecting your property, demonstrating dominance, or showing submission, the way that you fill your

space indicates your attitude. Touch an object and you're
saying, 'This is mine'. Turn away from it and you're saying,
'No, thanks'.

Demonstrating ownership

When you use your hands to lead and guide another person,
you're taking control. Your behaviour becomes dominant
as you touch what you consider to be yours. When you lead
another person by the hand, when you guide someone by
placing your hand on his back, or when you stand close to
your partner and put your hand on his upper arm, you're
demonstrating that you own that piece of property.

Victoria Beckham and Catherine Zeta Jones are masters of the
female proprietorial pose. When they stand close to their
husbands and place a hand on their man's chest or upper
arm, you can't misread the signal telling you that the man
belongs to them. Private property. Keep off.

Placing your hands on an object suggests a proprietorial
relationship with it. Even if you don't actually own the object,
by touching it you're establishing a dominant relationship
with that item. When you touch an object, you're indicating
that psychologically, if not in actual practice, you own, or are
in control of, the object.

James and his new bride, Beverly, went to a party of James's
work colleagues. Beverly knew very few people at the party.
Throughout the evening James frequently touched his wife,
as a sign of reassurance and of ownership. He guided her
through the room by placing his hand on her lower back, he
put his arm around her shoulders while introducing her to his
colleagues, and he often held her hand while they were in
conversation with other people.

Max's friend, JD, recently purchased his first car. He worked
hard and saved long to earn the money, and he's extremely
proud of the car, including its personalised licence plate and
alloy wheels. One day when he was at our home he asked
whether I'd take a photograph of him with his prized possession
standing in our drive. As JD stood next to his car, he placed
his hand on the bonnet for the first shot, and leaned against
the door for the second. Both positions indicate his strong
connection with the car and a real sense of his ownership of it.

Touching a person or an object implies that you've a relationship with that item. You can use this awareness to intimidate or dominate someone else, or you may observe someone trying to likewise intimidate or dominate you. Especially intimidating, for example, is when someone touches something that belongs to you.

If someone you don't know comes to your home or office, you can show ownership and dominance by leaning against your door frame in a proprietorial way.

Showing submission

Entering a foreign environment frequently causes people to feel uncomfortable and act in a submissive way. They wait to be invited to sit, refrain from touching objects in the space, and contain their gestures. Once they feel at ease, their body language opens up.

Amy's boss suggested that she attend one of our Positive Impact workshops. A potential high flyer, Amy's body language was letting her down. Although she was under consideration for promotion, her boss had concerns that when the time came, Amy wouldn't be able to fill her boss's shoes and move forward. Amy wasn't claiming her space. Her movements were hesitant, contained, and mostly close to her body. This behaviour, in combination with her slightly hunched shoulders, gave the impression of subservience. Working with recording equipment, Amy observed how her non-verbal behaviour was displaying her inner world of doubt and insecurity.

If you purposely want to show submission, close your body by pulling your arms in close to your body and keeping your hands to yourself.

Guarding your space

In addition to clarifying ownership of people and possessions, people jealously guard the space that immediately surrounds them. Humans create an invisible bubble around themselves in which they function. Placing objects between yourself and others, spreading your arms across your desk, and wrapping your arms around yourself are ways of guarding your personal space.

In normal circumstances most people respect one another's personal territory. Sometimes, however, space invasion is unavoidable. When an invasion of your space occurs, you feel uncomfortable. Another person entering your space can penetrate your guard. Fine, if you've invited that person in. Not so good if you neither know the person, nor want him there. Even when their personal space is invaded, people still find ways to limit the invasion as much as possible. Consider these examples:

- Turning your head away
- Avoiding eye contact
- Pulling into yourself

Beth was walking her dog, Bertie, along a country lane when Phillipa, a woman Beth knew and didn't much care for, pulled up next to them in her new Range Rover. 'Hello! Haven't seen you for ages,' Phillipa called out, jumping down from the car and giving Beth a hug. Grudgingly, Beth turned her head to avoid having to touch the woman's cheek with her own lips, and left her arms by her side, her excuse being that she was unable to let go of Bertie's lead. It wasn't until Phillipa had driven off that the stiffness around Beth's shoulders and neck was released, and she felt comfortable again.

Wait to be invited into the Close Intimate Zone to avoid causing offence, discomfort, or embarrassment.

Revealing comfort or discomfort

How near, how far, and at what angle you position yourself in relation to someone else, indicates how relaxed you feel with that person. Sitting comfortably amongst friends you probably sit close to one another. Your body leans towards them, and your eyes are engaged. Amongst people you prefer you weren't with, your body angles away. You avoid eye contact and you pull back. It's clear that you don't want to connect.

Putting distance and objects between yourself and another person can make for an awkward conversation. Stand too far away and you may come across as stand-offish. Get too close and you may be perceived as intrusive. Some people like to put objects and distance between themselves and others. It makes them feel protected and gives them the opportunity to observe someone from behind a barrier, whether actual or perceived. Others like to get up close right away. They want to burrow in and get connected.

If you turn your shoulder on another person you're showing him that you're not comfortable with him. Your shoulder acts as a barrier keeping the two of you at arms length. When someone turns his back on you, he's shutting you out.

One of the reasons that open-plan office workers put photographs, pot plants, and mascots on their computers is to put distance between themselves and others. When people are forced to sit close together they put up barriers in whatever way they can.

Open space between people can lead to accessibility. You sometimes see a person come from behind his desk to greet another without the desk acting like a barrier. Trainers, coaches, and teachers often prefer working in an open environment in order to connect with their listeners.

I recently ran a workshop in Portsmouth. Although scheduled to meet in one of the conference rooms, because of the large numbers who had signed up to attend, we had to relocate to the large, formal assembly theatre. As the delegates entered the room, I noticed they were heading toward the back, leaving rows of empty chairs between them and me. I already felt uncomfortable in this formal setting, and my vain attempts to close the gap fell on deaf ears. Several of the participants justified their position by saying that only senior managers and directors sit in the front rows. As the event was designed to be interactive it was vital that I connected with the delegates. I stepped down from the stage and walked amongst the group to break the ice and build the trust. After about 30 minutes the group began to move forward and spread themselves out around the room. A few of them even sat in the front row.

When your personal space is unavoidably infiltrated, such as in a crowded bus, and touching can't be escaped, only shoulders and upper arms should make contact. If the contact is any more intimate, people make an effort to move apart, in spite of the crowded conditions.

Maintaining your personal space

When strangers crowd in, you have to adjust your concept of how much space you need to conserve around you. Country people may initially feel quite uncomfortable in a large city. Where they're used to living in open spaces, they now find themselves confined within buildings. Crowded conditions take over where once there was distance. They may feel more constrained. Their gestures become fewer, smaller, and tighter as they adjust to their reduced space.

The next time you go to the doctor or hairdressers, observe where people sit. Normally you find a row of chairs for waiting clients. The first client usually sits at one end of the row. The next person to enter sits halfway down. Both are at a comfortable distance from one another – neither too close to cause discomfort nor too far away to appear standoffish. The next person sits at the other end, and the fourth person sits between the middle and end position, and so on until eventually someone is forced to sit next to another person.

When people queue in Britain they envelop themselves in an invisible space bubble. People have their own bubble and on a good day they respect one another's space. Interestingly, crowded conditions, such as those found on the rush hour bus, tube, or train, lead people to ignore one another. According to psychologist Robert Sommer, in crowded conditions people imagine that someone invading their personal space is inanimate. Therefore, no need exists to relay any social signals. Individuals stand or sit still when they're ignoring their surroundings. The larger the crowd, the less the individual body movement. People's faces take on a blank and expressionless look indicating that communication is not being sought. They avoid eye contact by staring at the ceiling or the floor.

Seating Arrangements

Seating positions should never happen by chance. When planning a dinner party or a special event, the hosts spend a great deal of energy deciding where their guests should sit. The position in which you're placed reflects your status, and impacts upon people's perception of you. Where other people place themselves in relation to you, signals their attitude toward you, their view of themselves in relation to you, and the level of cooperation you can expect from them.

Because rectangular tables enable people to have their own edges, equal space, and clear eye contact, everyone at the table can take a stance on a particular subject, although those at the shorter sides (the head) of the table are in a dominant position. Square tables are ideal for short, direct conversations. Round tables give everyone seated an equal amount of power and prominence.

Before you seat yourself, or direct people where you want them to sit, think about the outcome you want to have as a result of the people interacting.

Speaking in a relaxed setting

Sitting with the corner of a rectangular table between you and another person encourages relaxed, friendly conversation (see Figure 10-1). You can clearly see one another and open room exists for gesturing. The corner of the desk serves as a subtle barrier in case it's needed. This position also denotes an even division of space with both people on an equal footing.

Figure 10-1: Sitting in the corner position diffuses tension and promotes a positive attitude.

Cooperating

When you work on a task with another person, or if you find that you and someone else think along the same lines, you're more than likely to find yourselves sitting side by side. Most people intuitively sit in this configuration when they're working on a joint project with someone else. This position enables you to look easily at your partner. You can also reflect the other person's behaviour from this close position. You want to ensure that the person you're sitting next to doesn't feel that his space is being invaded.

When you introduce a third person to the cooperating position, the position in which you place yourself in relation to the other two determines how everyone at the table is perceived. By sitting next to the first person in the cooperating position, or at his side with the corner of the table between you, you're showing the new person that you and the first person are aligned. From this position you can speak and ask questions of the third person on the first person's behalf. In sales, this position is called 'siding with the opposition'.

Whenever you're influencing people, you should always aim to see their point of view, to make them feel at ease in your company, and to ensure that they feel good about working with you. You gain more cooperation by sitting in the corner, or cooperative position, than you do by placing yourself in the combative position, in which conversations are shorter and sharper.

Combating and defending

Placing yourself across a table from another person sets up a barrier and a hostile, or defensive, atmosphere. The barrier serves as a foundation upon which each side can take a firm stand and argue their point. Standing or sitting directly face to face with someone else indicates that a confrontation may be imminent. (When animals attack one another, they come in head to head.) A person under attack throws up a shield to defend himself. It can be as subtle as folding your hands at chest level, or as blatant as putting a Star Wars defence mechanism into action.

In a business scenario, sitting directly across the table from another person implies a competitive atmosphere. In a social situation, such as at a dinner party or in a restaurant, this position is viewed positively because it enables conversation.

If you want to reprimand someone in a work environment, or demonstrate that you're in charge, sit directly across your desk or table from the other person.

Research shows that managers who don't use their desks as a barrier are perceived as active listeners, fair-minded, and unlikely to show favouritism.

Keeping to yourself

If two people don't want to interact with one another they sit diagonally across the table, at the farthest ends of the table. This position is typical in a library, when two people share a reading table.

The expression 'diametrically opposed' comes from this seating position and implies lack of interest, indifference, or hostility. If you want to keep the discussions open between you and others, avoid sitting in this position.

Creating equality

King Arthur's Round Table empowered his knights with equal authority and status. No one was in a lesser, weaker, or more dominant position than anyone else. Each knight was able to claim the same amount of table territory as his compatriot, and everyone could be seen easily. The circle is considered a symbol of unity and strength, and sitting in a circle promotes this effect.

Although the model of King Arthur's round table promotes equality, who sits where in relation to the perceived leader denotes positions of status and power.

The position in which people sit affects the dynamics of a group's power. The people sitting on either side of the person of higher status (and holding the most power), hold the next level of power, the individual on the right of the high-status person being granted more power than the individual on the left. The farther away from the high-status individual, the more diminished the power. Whoever sits directly across from the person with the highest status is placed in the competitive position and is most likely to be the one who causes the most trouble.

In business, a rectangular desk is effectively used for business activities, short conversations, and reprimands. A round table creates an informal relaxed atmosphere. Square tables belong in the company cafeteria. High-status people sit facing the door, not with their backs to it.

If you're seated at a round table, having a discussion with two other people and you want to make sure that they're both involved, begin by ensuring that the three of you sit in a triangular position. When one person asks you a question, look at that person first as you begin to answer, and then turn your head towards the third person as you continue your answer. Carry on like this, turning your head back and forth between the two people as you complete your answer. As you make your final statement, complete your remarks by looking at the person who first posed the question. This technique makes both people feel included and is particularly useful in helping the second person to connect with you.

You can tell a family's distribution of power by the kind of dining table they have, as long as they were free to choose any shape table they wanted. Families that encourage their members to share their opinions and points of view, prefer round tables. Families with an authoritarian at the helm opt for rectangular tables.

Recently divorced, Anne was feeling shy, introverted, and somewhat unsure of herself. In spite of her lack of confidence, she accepted an invitation to a friend's dinner party. The hostess, knowing how Anne was feeling, seated her at the head of the table, facing into the room, with her back against the wall. Sitting in the most powerful position at the table, Anne found herself speaking throughout the evening with authority and confidence, and engaged comfortably with the people around her.

Orientating Yourself

Stand up, and you move and think one way. Lie down, and you think and move in another. Depending on whether you're standing to attention or slouching in your chair, you find yourself thinking and behaving differently. How you position yourself determines and sends out signals of how you view the world. The world, in turn, responds in its own way to the signals you send.

Horizontally

Someone who's lying out flat, or slumped over his desk, or is curled up in a ball, risks insulting his colleagues and companions. If the other people expect to demonstrate polite attentiveness, you're going to have to change your posture and show that you're alert.

If you're extremely dominant, or amongst exceptionally good friends in an informal setting, you can get away with being horizontal. In the first case, you don't care what people think and say, and in the second case you know that you're safe with friends and trusted family members.

People in a supine position find that their thinking process is expansive – their thoughts free to meander and flow. In an upright position, thoughts are sharper, clearer, and more coherent. You need both styles of thinking in order to explore all possibilities fully.

With the baby boomer and subsequent generations, people's posture has become more relaxed. Before World War II, people behaved more formally. Their clothes were structured and restrictive. After the war, fashions changed. With the advent of blue jeans as a wardrobe staple, our gestures and body placements reflect the new, relaxed atmosphere. People now move with more ease and less restriction because of the flexibility and freedom their clothes permit.

You need a partner to do this with. Ask the other person to lie on the floor while you stand over him, accentuating the height difference. Give the person lying on the floor as loud and powerful a telling off as you can. Change positions, with you now lying on the floor looking up at your partner standing over you. Repeat the reprimand. You find that your voice lacks force and you've no authority.

Vertically

A person positioning himself lower than you is demonstrating a subordinate position. Someone standing above you is sending dominant signals. Whether you position yourself high or low, you're telling people where you stand in the pecking order. Kings and Queens are referred to as 'Your Highness'. Crooks, robbers, and other unsavoury characters are labelled 'low life'. People talk about the 'upper classes' and the 'lower classes'. The higher up you go, the more perceived status and authority you have. The lower down the scale, the less influence you wield.

Lowering yourself

In order to make himself appear small and deferential, a man removes his hat or tips his head when meeting someone in a position of higher authority. Women curtsey, in a sign of deference and respect when meeting royalty. Men and women genuflect or bow their heads upon entering a church, and kneel for prayer. Beggars sit on the ground. When their eyes look downwards, they're at their lowest.

Short people suffer the indignity of being looked down upon. Because they're shorter than others, their credibility often gets overlooked. Short women are particularly susceptible to interruption and being talked over in meetings. In order to make up for their lack of height, short people must gesture and behave with strength, command authority, and demonstrate gravitas. Filling their space by standing up, holding their arms slightly away from their bodies, and gesturing with clarity and focus, creates an image of confidence, control, and commitment.

The more subordinate a person feels, the lower he positions his body.When a student or employee enters your office and you sit while he stands, you're demonstrating your power. The commanding officer doesn't rise when the junior lieutenant enters the Officers' Mess.

Sometimes, lowering yourself can raise your status. When you flop into a chair in someone else's home in front of the owner who's standing, you're demonstrating your comfort in that person's territory. By touching his belongings and behaving in unrestricted ways you're indicating that although someone else may have a claim on the environment, you're more than comfortable taking over. This behaviour can be perceived as dominant or even aggressive.

Japanese businesses instruct staff members to bow at different angles, depending on the status of the customer. A customer who's 'browsing' receives a 15-degree bow whereas the customer who wants to buy is awarded up to a 45-degree bow.

Elevating yourself

An Olympic gold medallist stands on a podium above the other medal winners and the judge sits above his court. To live in the penthouse is to live above, and look down upon, the crowd. People in 'high places' are looked up to and seen as superior. It would be most unusual to find the senior partner's or chief executive's office in the basement.

Look at the person sitting at the head of the table and you're likely to be looking at the boss.

Clients frequently ask me how they can project an elevated image when they're not tall. One female client who is just barely above 5 feet in her stocking feet tells me that she pretends that she's tall. Instead of straining and struggling to gain attention, she puts her efforts into visualising herself as a tall, slim woman, who fills her space and commands attention. By acting the part, she radiates the appearance.

Many of my clients work in the public arena and frequently appear on television. One of my shorter clients consistently received feedback that, although he was knowledgeable, on camera he lacked credibility and gravitas. Reviewing his tapes together, I devised a strategy for future public appearances to assure increased authority and presence: His lectern was to be customised in order that his chest was visible, and cameras were to be angled upwards, to give him the appearance of greater height. I coached him in speaking directly to the camera so that his viewing public felt that he was speaking to them individually. I put him in dark, single-breasted suits that elongated his body. His television performances improved dramatically. One observer reported that he had a new sense of gravitas and positive impact.

To project authority, inflate your chest, stand tall, and look people directly in the eye. Stand in a meeting to gain attention and control.

Asymmetrically

If you're sitting at your desk and one hand is resting on your desk and your other hand is placed on your hip, you're sitting in an *asymmetrical pose*. Unlike a symmetrical pose in which corresponding body parts mirror one another, the asymmetrical position is two different poses. One side of your body is in one position while the other side is in another.

Straight posture commands respect and authority. Asymmetrical positions hold intrigue. They reveal more about the person. A man standing stiffly upright, with his mouth closed, and his eyes staring straight ahead is giving little away. Someone whose body has fluidity and movement is more expressive. When your torso and limbs are in contrasting positions, they create impact and interest.

Chapter 11

Dating and Mating

. . . .

In This Chapter

▶ Attracting someone's attention

▶ Showing that you're interested

▶ Progressing through the romance

. . . .

*T*ry flirting without using body language. Go on, give it a go. Surprise, surprise! It can't be done. You simply can't convey romantic interest without the body getting into the act. To play a really successful game of flirtation your body must speak what your mouth mustn't say.

If you're feeling good about yourself the way you focus your eyes, position your mouth, and manoeuvre your shoulders, hips, and hands send out signals that say, 'Check me out! I think you're hot!' After you get your target's attention you shift gears to hold onto his or her interest and move the attraction to another level. Finally, having captured and conquered the unsuspecting, or equally interested party, your body moves into a new mode of behaving that demonstrates comfort, ease, and familiarity. Observe how long-term lovers anticipate one another's actions by the way they move in synch with their partners.

How you use your body exposes how ready you are for a bit of romance, how attractive you feel, and how interested you are. Some courtship signals are deliberate, others are unconscious. In this chapter I explore the wide, wild world of courtship behaviour and see how it can put a big smile on your face.

Attracting Someone's Attention

Watch a person in the company of someone he or she finds attractive and see what happens. The stomach gets pulled in, whether it needs to be or not, slumping is exchanged for an upright stance, displays of health and vitality are conveyed through a lively walk, muscle tone becomes heightened, and a youthful appearance replaces the ravages of time or too many late nights.

Men stand taller, thrust up their chins, and expand their chests, making them look like the king of the jungle. Women tilt their heads, flick their hair, and expose their wrists and necks, demonstrating vulnerability and submissiveness. Your eyes dilate if you find another person attractive. And you can do nothing to stop it. If things go to plan, the recipient of your gaze unconsciously responds in a similar way and the excitement begins.

Vickie is a particularly attractive woman. A former model, she has kept her figure trim and fit, wears just enough make up to highlight her perfectly formed features, and moves with purpose and energy. One day Vickie and I went out to brunch. As she walked through the restaurant I noticed a man tracking her while continuing his conversation with his partner. Although he didn't move his head, the muscles around his mouth raised, he slightly adjusted his seating position while expanding his chest, his eyes widened, and he watched her out of the corner of his eye until she had passed. Once she was out of his line of vision his body reverted to its original position and he continued his conversation as if nothing had happened.

Christine was strolling along the beach one afternoon not paying much attention to herself or the other people until she noticed coming towards her a very fit, handsome young man. Without thinking she immediately adjusted her posture by pulling in her stomach, squaring her shoulders, and straightening her back. Her energy heightened, she flicked her hair off her face, and put a spring into her step. As they got closer to one another, she noticed that the man had also adjusted his posture and by the time they were close enough to see each other fully they looked one another in the eye and smiled. Christine may have allowed her interest to take her to the next step of engaging him in conversation if she hadn't remembered that she had a handsome young husband waiting for her at home.

When you're rating someone's attractiveness and in turn are being rated, messages that convey interest, keenness, and compatibility are constantly being relayed. No matter how old, fit, or capable people are, they're all checking each other out.

Here are some things to keep in mind as you go courting:

- ✓ **Women usually make the first move:** Research shows that 90 per cent of the time women initiate the first move in the mating game. I can hear my mother now: 'Nice girls don't show that they're interested. They wait for the man to make the first move.' Well, apparently not. Women go for it. Men simply respond. Women send out a series of subtle movements to the man she's lined up in her sights. If she's good at it the man thinks that he's taking the lead although in fact he's just dancing to her tune.

  If a woman is to succeed in the ritual she has to count on the man to decode the signals she sends out. She must then respond to the signs he sends back in a way that gives him the green light to move to the next stage. For a man to succeed in this game he has to be able to read the signals correctly.

- ✓ **Men aren't very good at reading the signals properly:** Men tend to misinterpret friendly behaviour for sexual interest because men have 10 to 20 times more testosterone than women.

- ✓ **Availability counts more than beauty:** Men pursue a woman who may not be the most sexually attractive as long as she gives off availability signals. A beautiful woman with all the right physical attributes is left on the shelf if she doesn't appear to be interested. In a contest between looks and signals, signals win hands down.

Going courting: The five stages

When you see someone you want to get to know better, the first order of business is to get that person's attention.

You go through a predictable pattern to the courtship sequence when you see someone you think is cute, hunky, or simply appealing:

1. **Eye contact.**

   The woman looks across a crowded room. She spots a man she finds attractive. She waits for him to notice her. She focuses her eyes on his for three–five seconds and then looks away. He watches to see what she does next. She looks at him again, and at least one more time. When a man sees a woman who catches his eye he glances at her body first. After he makes eye contact with her he slightly narrows his eyes and holds the gaze somewhat longer than he normally would, indicating his interest.

2. **Smile.**

   The woman flashes a fleeting smile or two. This is a hint of a smile with a promise of things to come rather than a toothy grin. It's important that the man responds to this signal or else the woman will think that he's not interested and will move her sights. A man establishes eye contact with a woman and lifts his chin slightly as he smiles, inviting her to engage with him.

3. **Preen.**

   The muscles of both men and women become slightly tensed. Her posture straightens, accentuating her physical attributes. If seated, she crosses her legs to show them off. If she's standing she shifts her hips and tilts her head to expose her neck. She plays with her hair, runs her tongue over her lips, and adjusts her clothes and jewellery. A man may straighten his stance, pull in his stomach, push out his chest, adjust his clothes, and touch his hair. Both point their bodies towards one another.

4. **Talk.**

   The man walks over to the woman, making it look as though he's the initiator, and gives her a few chat-up lines. Having given him permission to approach by the signals she's sent through her body language, a woman then waits for the man to begin the conversation.

Actually initiating a conversation can be a minefield. Here are a couple of tips to help you navigate it safely:

- If you misread the signal and sense that the approach is going to land you where you'd rather not be, pretend that you just want to ask the other person about unrelated subjects. You may sound a bit of an idiot but at least you aren't given a brusque brush off in response to a clumsy pass.

- If after a few minutes of speaking with a woman she yawns, frowns, or sneers you can count on the fact that she's not interested. If she crosses her arms, puts her hands in her pockets, and avoids your gaze, you may as well walk away.

5. **Touch.**

If a woman's still interested she'll seek an opportunity to lightly touch the man's arm accidentally on purpose, or with a genuine reason. If both people are happy with the touching process they'll increase the amount. An easy way to move to the touching stage is by shaking hands. Touching a person's hand is more intimate than touching an arm.

You may not have thought that so much choreography exists in the initial stages of courtship and the steps may seem incidental. They're not. Without going through these five stages, which may only take a few moments at most, the courting ritual stops before it begins.

Highlighting gender differences

People who want to attract the attention of the opposite sex emphasise their gender to make themselves sexually attractive and appealing. Women pout, arch their backs, and lean forward, bringing their arms close to their bodies to push their breasts together to create a deep and appealing cleavage. Men stand tall, expand their chests, and hook their thumbs over their waistbands or into their trouser pockets with their fingers exposed to subtly point towards their nether regions.

Unless you want to be perceived as a hot totty or aggressively on the make, keep your gestures muted in the early stages of the courtship process. Otherwise you may find your signs of possible interest being interpreted as signals of immediate availability.

Walking, wiggling, and swaggering

The way you walk reveals your interest. Both men and women take on youthful characteristics when seeking the other's attention. They create the impression that they have an unlimited source of energy by the way they vigorously bounce along. Unlimited energy can be very sexy because it indicates the promise of being a tireless mate.

A woman rolls her hips and swings her arms further back, exposing her soft and supple flesh. Because women have wider hips than men as well as a wider crotch gap between their legs they are able to walk with a rolling motion that draws attention to the pelvic area. Men, being built differently, can't emulate this walk and find the difference sexually appealing. If you've ever seen the film *Some Like It Hot* you're sure to remember the scene where Marilyn Monroe walks down the railway platform, while Jack Lemmon and Tony Curtis stare at her undulating bottom in awe. As Jack Lemmon says, this remarkable movement was 'like Jell-o on springs'.

Advertisers regularly use this rolling gesture in their campaigns to sell their products. Women want to be like the model and men want to have her. Either way creates increased product awareness, which is all the advertiser cares about.

If you're a man, you swagger, which makes you look strong and domineering. You swing your arms across your body, elbows bent, hands at waist height, and turn your arms inward showing just how manly you are.

Filling the space

Men adopt dominant positions by sitting with their legs apart and their arms opened to show they need lots of space for their frames to fit into. They shift their bodies, change their positions, and use their hands frequently to emphasise what they're saying.

Women accentuate their femininity by moving slowly and pulling their gestures towards themselves. They give the appearance of needing less space, not more. Submissive gestures like tilting their heads, crossing their ankles and legs as well as touching their hair and face indicate that they're ready, willing, and able.

If a man and woman find each other attractive their bodies lean towards each another.

Other stuff

The clothes you wear and the way you wear them advertise your sexual availability. How much of your body you show and which parts are on display, as well as your facial expressions, also send signals as to your attraction and willingness to move forward:

- ✔ **Facial expressions:** Women use lively and animated facial expressions demonstrating interest, vitality, and energy. Men's expressions are more controlled reflecting their dominance, restraint, and power.

- ✔ **Clothing:** In addition to protecting you from the elements, your choice of clothing signals what you want to reveal about yourself. In response, people make assumptions about you based on what you wear. Clothes that draw attention to your sexuality indicate that you're prepared to be noticed. Low-slung or tight jeans draw the eye to the wearer's genitalia whereas tight-fitting tops enhance the chest.

Showing That You're Free

Having established that you're interested in the other person, it's time for you to show that you're available. Some of the gestures you use are studied and deliberate. Others are completely unconscious. They all have the effect of showing that you're in place and ready to go.

Although men and women use the same basic preening gestures like touching their hair, smoothing their clothes, pointing their bodies in the other's direction, and increasing eye contact, some subtle differences are worth noting.

Unlike most of the mammal population where the males are in charge of sexual advertising, in the world of humans, women usually take the lead. They use clothes, hairstyles, make-up, and fragrance to advertise their femininity. Whether a conscious choice or not, an interested and available woman sends out signals designed to lure a man into her fold.

Courting gestures of women

The list of female sexual behaviours is long and moves right down her body from her head to the tips of her toes.

Tossing your head and flicking your hair

When a woman sees a man she finds attractive she unconsciously tosses her head or runs her fingers through her hair. Whether her hair is long or short the gesture is a subtle way of showing that she cares about her appearance and is making an effort to look appealing.

An added benefit of this movement is that it exposes her soft underarm, a highly sensual part of a woman's body that most men find irresistible (see Figure 11-1).

Canting your head

A head tilted to the side gives an appealing and helpless look (see Figure 11-2). By exposing the neck, a vulnerable part of the body, the head-cant is an ideal courtship signal because it implies that the woman trusts the man so much she is prepared to display a defenceless part of her body to him.

The origins of the head-cant can be traced to infancy. A baby rests its head on the parents' shoulders when being comforted. The head-cant is a stylised version of the infant's gesture and unconsciously sends out an appeal for protection. Without knowing why, men feel a sudden surge of compassion, probably because the woman looks so vulnerable and helpless when she adopts this pose.

Figure 11-1: The hair toss and underarm display are enticing.

Figure 11-2: The head-cant demonstrates vulnerability and elicits protective feelings.

Showing your neck

A woman uses two ways to expose her neck to make herself look appealing. In one she raises her chin slightly; in the other she turns her head so the man can get a clear view of her neck. Either way, by showing her soft skin on a vulnerable part of her body, she makes herself look helpless and sexy. A lethal combination no hot-blooded male can resist.

Dipping the head

One way a woman can make her eyes seem bigger, and herself seem smaller, is to lower her head when she's looking up at her lover. The result is that she looks vulnerable and in need of protection. Women also lower their heads when they're flirting with a man because it's a sign of submission.

Pouting and wetting your lips

Full lips are seen as a female characteristic and are considered full of sexual promise. When a woman pouts, the size of the lips increase, as does the man's interest.

The facial bone structure of men and women is vastly different. During the teen years, as testosterone increases in men, their features become stronger, larger, and more pronounced. Women's facial features change only slightly. Due to more subcutaneous fat, their faces seem full and childlike, particularly their lips.

Touching yourself

Women have a much larger number of nerve sensors than men, making them more sensitive to touching sensations. Women leisurely stroke their necks, throats, and thighs signalling to a man that if he plays his cards right she just may let him caress her in a similar way. By touching herself a woman can fantasise about how it would feel if the man she fancies were the one doing the touching.

Touching yourself draws attention to that part of your body and gets another person thinking about what it would feel like to be the person touching you. Often you're not aware that you're touching or stroking yourself. The gesture is an unconscious action in response to your interest in the other person. Women who *are* aware of the effect this behaviour elicits become adept at performing self-touching actions to call attention to themselves.

Exposing your wrists

The underside of the wrist is considered to be one of the most erotic places on a woman's body. This is probably because the skin there is highly delicate. A woman showing interest and availability reveals this smooth, soft skin, increasing the rate of frequency as her interest grows (see Figure 11-3).

Figure 11-3: Exposed wrists are a sign of availability.

Fondling cylindrical objects

If you find yourself fondling any object that remotely resembles a phallus, you are acting out what's going on inside your head.

Don't be surprised if the man you're speaking with fondles a personal item of yours while you fiddle with your earring, pen, or the stem of your glass. The stimulus is too much for him to resist and he has to respond in a similar way to show he's paying attention and wants to possess you.

Sliding a ring on and off your finger can show a desire to have sex with the person you're speaking to.

Glancing sideways over a raised shoulder

A woman who raises her shoulder is performing an act of self-mimicry by using her shoulder to emulate her rounded breasts. By turning her shoulder towards a man, holding his gaze with slightly lowered eyelids just long enough to get his attention, and then quickly looking away, a woman can drive a man to distraction (see Figure 11-4). If he's interested, that is. This gesture tantalises the man and suggests a peep show which most men find hard to resist.

Figure 11-4: A raised shoulder highlights a woman's roundness and curv

Putting your handbag in close proximity

A woman's handbag is her personal domain. Even most married men live in terror of entering this most forbidden territory. Because a woman treats her handbag as if it were a personal extension of her body, it becomes a strong signal o sexual intimacy when she places her bag close to a man.

If a woman finds a man attractive she may deliberately stroke and caress her bag in an inviting manner, tantalising and teasing her male admirer.

A woman who places her handbag close enough to a man for him to see or touch it is sending out signals that she's attracted to him. If she keeps her bag away from him, she's creating an emotional distance.

Pointing your knee in his direction

Watch the direction a woman's knee points when she sits with one leg tucked under the other. If a man is at the end of the sight line you can bet she finds him interesting. From this relaxed position, she's able to flash a bit of thigh and gain her target's attention.

Dangling a shoe

If a woman is sitting with a man and dangles a shoe off the end of her foot she's sending out the message that she's relaxed and comfortable in his company. In addition, the foot acts like a phallus as it thrusts itself in and out of her shoe. Many men become unsettled by this gesture and they don't know why.

If you want to test a woman's comfort level as she swings her dangling shoe off her pedicured toes, say or do something that unsettles her or makes her anxious and observe how quickly that shoe goes back on her foot.

Entwining your legs

Men consistently rank the leg twine as the most appealing sitting position a woman can take. Women consciously use this gesture to draw attention to their legs. When one leg is pressed up against the other it gives the appearance of highly toned muscles (see Figure 11-5), which is the position the body takes just before engaging in sex.

Women who want to entice a man and demonstrate their own interest slowly cross and uncross their legs and gently stroke their thighs as an indication of their desire to be caressed. Think of Sharon Stone's provocative leg cross in the film *Basic Instinct*.

Figure 11-5: Men rank the leg twine as number one for its appeal.

Courting gestures of men

Compared with the vast amount of courtship signals women possess, men have a sad and paltry few. In their effort to attract a woman, men often rely on their power, money, and status as a means of flexing their muscles. Men's idea of a sexual invitation is to rev their engines, flaunt their wealth, and challenge other men.

This is not to say that men don't preen when a potential partner comes into view. In addition to pulling in his stomach, expanding his chest, and lifting his head like a conquering hero, a man smoothes his hair, straightens his tie, adjusts his clothes, and flicks real or imaginary dust from his lapel.

If you're a man and you want to see whether a woman finds you attractive, tidy up your appearance by wearing a smart suit or a jacket and tie. A tie that is loosely knotted and slightly off centre elicits a nurturing response in a woman. She instinctively reaches out to make the necessary adjustments, brushing your shoulder or lapel just in case a bit of fluff needs removing. If she's drawn to you, she wants to make you look like the perfect man she hopes you are.

About the most sexually aggressive posture a man can display is where he tucks his thumbs into his belt or the top of his pockets. With his arms in the ready position and his fingers pointing to his genital area, men take this stance to stake their claim or show other men they're not to be messed about. If a man uses this gesture in front of a woman he's indicating that he's both dominant and virile.

If a woman sees a man with his thumbs in his pockets and his fingers pointing toward his crotch combined with dilated pupils, a longer-than-usual gaze, and one foot pointed toward her, she's on a winner if she guesses he's displaying interest in her.

In the 15th century, the male codpiece was introduced. The purpose of this not-so-subtle item of clothing was to display the purported size of the man's penis, which determined his social status. New Guinea male natives still display their penises, while Western men do so more subtly by wearing tight-fitting jeans, pocketsize swimsuits, or dangling a bunch of keys in their nether regions. By having something to fondle or hold onto in front of his crotch, a man has the perfect excuse to put his hands down there to make any necessary adjustments. Whereas a woman would never put her hands on her genitals in public, even if she did have an itch down there, it's quite normal and acceptable, at least on the sports field, for a man to do just that.

A universal sign of attraction: Dilated pupils

Anyone who has ever gazed longingly into another person's eyes knows how powerfully the eyes convey the message that says, 'I find you incredibly attractive.' What you may not realise is that your pupils dilate when something arouses and stimulates you. As you can do nothing to control this reaction give up playing hard to get because anyone paying close attention sees your pupils enlarging and knows they're in with a chance.

If you want to kick-start a romance, arrange to meet your person of choice in a dimly lit place. Both your and your partner's pupils dilate because of the lack of light, creating the impression that you're interested in one another. The rest is up to you.

For more information on what messages you can send with a gaze alone, go to Chapter 5.

Progressing Through the Romance

The courtship procedure is made up of a series of stages, as explained in the section, 'Going courting: The five stages' earlier in this chapter. In the early stages of courtship a woman may position herself to indicate that she's interested and available. A man may stroke a woman's hand to show he wants physical intimacy. Depending on how each person reacts to the other's signals, the courtship progresses or comes to a screeching halt. If you find yourself laughing, tickling, and generally engaging in playful behaviour when you're with Cute Guy or Gorgeous Gal, you know you're at least 'in like' if not yet 'in love' with one another. Goofing around and acting like puppies in a basket is harmless, unthreatening behaviour that allows you to show one another your nurturing and loving sides.

Matching each other's behaviours

The closer two people are emotionally the more similar their postures are. Certain postures and emotions are linked, so when two people adopt the same physical position they're probably experiencing similar feelings. Observe a couple who are in tune with one another and you can see that their movements are coordinated and their postures match.

Showing that you belong together

People who establish a physical closeness give the impression that they're emotionally close as well. A man may put his arm around a woman's waist or shoulders, sending out the message that she's his woman. A woman may remove a piece of fluff from her man's jacket or straighten his tie, giving the message to anyone who's watching that he belongs to her.

Other signs of togetherness are linking arms or holding hands while you're walking with your partner. The main reason people hold onto one another this way is not to keep from falling over but to show that they're connected.

When you hold hands, your hand may be in front, or behind; how the hands are positioned can indicate who's in charge. Usually the man's hand is in front with his palm facing towards the back. It's not known if this happens because men are taller or because they like to lead from the front. If a woman has her hand in the front position it's usually because she's taller than her partner and finds it uncomfortable to put her hand in the back position. If she's shorter than her man and still puts her hand in front, however, it's because she likes to be in charge, regardless of the physical discomfort it may cause both her and her partner. For more about what certain hand movements and positions mean, go to Chapter 8.

After the inauguration of George W. Bush in 2001, Hillary and Bill Clinton left the ceremony walking hand in hand. Bill looked composed and in control and Hillary looked supportive. Photos and film coverage show that Hillary was holding Bill's hand with her hand in the front position. The difference in their heights and the male-female relationship would have dictated the opposite position. However, what was clearly demonstrated was that Hillary, not Bill, was the person in charge.

Chapter 12

Crossing the Cultural Divide

● ●

In This Chapter

▶ Greeting people and saying farewell

▶ Understanding different cultures

▶ Playing by the rules

● ●

*W*ith businesses spanning the globe, students travelling the world, and the media bringing foreign lands into people's homes on a daily basis, no group can any longer believe in the infallibility of their own customs and culture. As the singer/songwriter Paul Simon says, 'One man's ceiling is another man's floor.'

In spite of the shrinking world, or perhaps because of it, cultures hold onto their customs and traditions with pride and determination. Behaviours as simple as counting on your fingers, walking along the street, and shaking hands, vary widely across the globe.

Unless you know the rules that govern behaviour in cultures other than your own, you can make some major mistakes that, in addition to insulting your host, may lead to a diplomatic crisis. Or, at least an uncomfortable embarrassment.

You don't want to make a fool of yourself, insult your host, or cause an international crisis because you didn't know the differences between acceptable and unacceptable behaviours. So when in doubt, ask. A native is more than happy to guide you in the ways of her country and is flattered that you asked. One gesture that you're always safe to use, no matter where you go, is the smile. This is the one truly universal gesture that's understood by the most sophisticated city person as well as by desert nomads.

Because so many countries and cultures exist in the world, and I have so few pages in which to write about them, this chapter gives you a few tips and techniques to get you started on a safe path as you trek the globe.

Greetings and Farewells

Whether you kiss, bow, or shake hands when you greet someone and bid her farewell, how you do so indicates your culture's attitude toward bodily contact. In some countries the standard practice is to touch, whereas other cultures view touching as rude and highly intrusive. In some countries men and women are even forbidden to touch in public. To break that taboo can cause, if not an international crisis, a major upset between the families.

Expecting to be touched

If you've ever travelled to Latin lands, from South America to the Mediterranean, you know that the people are comfortable with getting up close and personal. Big hugs and planting kisses on your friends' and family's cheeks are the norm.

Colleagues walking down the street hand in hand or with their arms intertwined or draped over one another's shoulders implies nothing more than friendship. Public displays of affection are standard practice and are to be expected.

The following are a few examples of the types of greetings you can expect in various regions of the world:

- **In France:** If you make friends with a French person, expect her to kiss your cheeks three times when you say hello and goodbye.

- **In Brazil:** Upon greeting and departure, the custom is to shake hands with everyone present in a group. Once a friendship has been established, expect to be embraced.

  Brazilian women exchange kisses on alternating cheeks: Twice if they're married, three times if they're single. The third kiss is to ensure 'good luck' in finding a spouse.

✔ **In the Middle East and Gulf States:** Touching upon greeting in the Middle Eastern and the Gulf States is common. Wait for your counterpart to initiate the exchange because several styles of greeting are used.

In Saudi Arabia be prepared to go through an elaborate greeting ritual with another person. Although a Westernised Saudi man shakes hands with another man, the customary Saudi greeting between men is a more complicated affair. After saying the traditional 'salaam alaykum' you shake hands and say 'kaif halak'. Then you and your Saudi counterpart put your left hands on the other's right shoulders and kiss one another on each cheek. Finally, your new-found friend takes your hand in his. Unless, of course, you're a woman, in which case no bodily contact is involved at all. (So if you're a woman, don't be offended if a Saudi man doesn't shake your hand.)

Personal distance between speakers is close in the Middle East, so backing away can be interpreted as an insult. Be prepared for more touching and physical contact in conversations. In fact, for Arab men holding hands is quite common – the gesture is a sign of friendship and respect.

Traditionally, a veiled Saudi woman in the company of a Saudi man isn't introduced.

Shortly after Charlotte, her husband, and their two young children moved to Saudi Arabia, they visited the Red Sea for a bit of swimming and sightseeing. When they arrived, Charlotte noticed that the men were chatting, embracing, swimming, and seemed to be having a grand time. The women, covered from head to foot in dark, heavy, traditional dress, clustered in the background, looking after the children when needed. The men were such a close, personal group that the women and children seemed extraneous to their needs. With her western frame of mind, Charlotte resented the men 'having all the fun'. She later found out from a Saudi friend that many women have their own very close and intimate friendships at home and out of the public eye. They are equally warm and expressive in private, whereas in public, they're more reserved and contained.

The standard Asian handshake is more of a handclasp. It lasts between 10–12 seconds and is rather limp. This contrasts with the North American handshake that lasts approximately 3–4 seconds and is firm.

The Chinese are more comfortable greeting another person with a handshake than in many other Far Eastern countries. A slight nod or bow is also a proper form for greetings and departures. Wait for them to initiate the gesture and follow their lead. However, the Chinese don't like being touched by people they don't know. This is especially true of older people and individuals in important positions. If in doubt, leave out the double-handed handshake.

Acknowledging the no-touching rule

Although in many Far Eastern countries, people greet one another by shaking hands, the Japanese have an aversion to informal bodily contact. Japanese doing business in the West force themselves to shake hands although they may feel uncomfortable doing so. In their own country, the usual form of greeting is a long, low bow from the waist and a formal exchange of business cards. Though young people are defying the norms of their parents, be aware that the Japanese traditionally disapprove of male-female touching in public.

If you feel awkward bowing to a Japanese colleague or customer, seeing it as a sign of subservience, do it anyway. That is, if you want to make a favourable impression. What you are saying by this gesture is that you value that person's experience and wisdom. Never put your hand or hands in your pockets when you're bowing, shaking hands, or giving a speech because doing so is considered to be extremely rude in Japan.

Cities in Japan are crowded places. You may need to push through the throngs, as the Japanese do. This is done by holding your hand in front of your face, with bent elbow, rather like a child pretending to be a shark, or like a Karate chop, while bowing and saying 'excuse me'.

When presenting your business card to a Japanese person hold it with both your hands and present it with your details facing toward the other person.

A word about waving farewell

The simple act of waving someone goodbye isn't so simple after all. What you think of as a simple wave may be interpreted as an offensive gesture.

Most Europeans face their palms front and wag their fingers up and down with their arm stretched forward and held stationary. Americans hold their palms forward with their arms outstretched and wave their hand back and forth from side to side. Throughout most of Europe this gesture would be interpreted as 'no' except in Greece, where the gesture is highly insulting and you can easily find yourself pleading innocence to the local authorities.

Higher and Lower Status Behaviour

Across cultures and continents, people of lower status demonstrate deference to the person holding the higher status.

Status behaviour is about showing respect. Around the world people, in varying degrees, demonstrate deference to people who are older, wiser, and in positions of authority. Usually, to show respect you put yourself in a lower position to the other person. At other times you stand to attention to show respect.

Within royal households, staff bow or curtsey when the monarch passes. In the military the enlisted soldiers stand to attention when the commanding officer enters a barracks. School students are taught to rise when an adult enters the classroom and when the boss struts through the office the staff straighten up. In Japan and other Asian countries subordinates don't look their superiors in the eye, whereas in Western cultures eye contact is the norm.

Bowing, kneeling, and curtseying

Bowing, kneeling, curtseying, and lowering the head are low status behaviours. By curling up the body and lowering it, you make yourself look small in relation to another person. This behaviour can be traced to the animal kingdom where creatures under attack cringe and crouch to protect themselves.

In Japan you can tell a person's status in relation to another's by how long and low she bows. Someone holding a lower status bows lower and longer. If equals are bowing to one another they match one another's bows. If one of the people wants to show more respect she adds an extra bow. The Japanese also add another bow for someone who is much older, as well as for a customer whose business they are hoping to get.

 When you're bowing to someone who holds a higher rank than you, make sure that you out bow her and keep your eyes respectfully lowered. If you're unsure of who holds the higher status, bow slightly less low than the other person. When bowing to a Japanese person your hands slide down the front of your legs towards your knees, or down the sides of your legs. Your back and neck is held stiffly and your eyes are averted.

 If you're ever reprimanded in front of someone in a higher position of authority make yourself look small. By showing deference you may calm troubled waters.

Standing to attention

Standing with a straight back, legs close together with your weight distributed evenly between them, arms by your sides, and your hands remaining still, is a sign of deference. If you've ever been called into the head teacher's office, stood up in court, or served in the military you know the position. You look straight ahead and don't move a muscle until you're spoken to.

My sister Paula and I were taught from an early age to stand up when an adult entered the room. We were also taught to look her in the eye, shake hands firmly, and say a polite 'hello'. This rule also applied when we were dining out and an adult stopped by the table to say hello. When we became adults, we were permitted to remain seated, although the men at the table were expected to stand. To this day, I still feel compelled to stand when an older person enters a room. This was a sign of respect and always brought parental approval.

Positioning and Setting Boundaries

In some countries the common and expected behaviour is for people to stand close to each other, whereas in others a wide berth between people is the norm. For example, in Argentina people stand close to one another. If you back away they may think that you're shy and move closer to fill the gap. Australians, however, require a lot of space between themselves – if you get closer than an arm's length away an Aussie feels hemmed in.

Visit the Nordic countries and you may notice similarities in the way people move in relation to one another. What the well-trained eye notices is that they're all quite restrained in the way they use their bodies. As opposed to their southern cousins, who embrace public physicality, they shy away from effusive gestures, and consider hugging to be taboo.

If you want to avoid embarrassing your Nordic friend or acquaintance, particularly in public, refrain from behaving in an intimate manner. Save your hugs for home.

If you were a fly on the wall in an American manufacturing company you'd see the plant manager walking around, chatting informally with the staff and factory workers. The manager may be dressed in a suit for a business meeting, or more casually if not. In France, by contrast, the plant manager always wears a suit and begins the day by greeting everyone in the office and in the factory with a handshake. This shows the hierarchic style of the French company, whereas the American plant has a flatter management structure.

In many Western cultures, when friends greet each other, you may see them perform the 'air kiss', shown in Figure 12-1, in which a kiss to the right and left cheeks is directed towards the sky rather than landing on the face.

Figure 12-1: The air kiss is a form of greeting that doesn't require much contact.

Like southern Europeans and unlike their Japanese neighbours, the Chinese demonstrate their regard for members of their own sex by publicly holding hands or making other forms of physical contact. Opposite sexes don't engage in public displays of affection.

Common Gestures, Multiple Interpretations

Just when you thought you knew the meaning of laughter, the 'thumbs up' sign, and giving the 'okay' signal, you find yourself creating the most embarrassing faux pas. All you can plead is ignorance. Hardly a viable excuse.

Thumbs up

The thumbs up sign means different things in different cultures. In many cultures it means 'good'. Even in those cultures where thumbs up means the same as it does in the 'home' culture – like Britain and America – how it's given is important.

If you're travelling in Japan and want to indicate that everything's just great, stick your thumb up in the air with a clenched fist. However, the same gesture in the Arab world is viewed as a major misdemeanour and can therefore land you in big trouble.

The 'okay' sign

Traveller, beware. North Americans make a circle with their index finger and thumb, the other fingers slightly raised, to indicate approval (see Figure 12-2). When the Japanese make this sign they're signalling money. You're regarded as vulgar if you make this sign in Brazil. Whereas, for the French, the gesture stands for zero.

 Ask your host, or read ahead of time, what the okay sign means in a particular country. In Arab countries it's a rude sexual gesture. So, don't assume that it means the same thing universally. Giving the okay sign can be a blessing or a curse!

Never give the okay sign in Japan while shaking your fist – it's considered to be an extremely rude gesture.

Laughter

When a person laughs in the Western world, you're safe in assuming that they're happy. If you hear the same laughter – with a slightly different accent – in Japan, don't think that everything's fine. Japanese laugh as a means of controlling their displeasure. Laughter also conceals embarrassment, confusion, and shock, and isn't only a gesture used for mirth.

Figure 12-2: Be careful where you choose to use the okay sign.

Cultures have personalities, like people. Some are open, outgoing, and extrovert. Others are less expressive, and their gestures are fewer, closer to the body and generally more restrained. Sit in a restaurant in Rome and watch the people laughing, interrupting one another, and touching a lot. Take yourself to Stockholm and experience the difference. People are quiet, more contained in their gestures, and demonstrate less emotion. Both groups are equally friendly and caring; they express their feelings and good will quite differently.

Laughter is associated with humour. Have you ever watched the same film in two different countries with different national audiences? I remember watching the film *Four Weddings and a Funeral* both in Britain and in America. The two audiences laughed at different places.

A young Japanese woman reveals her embarrassment by giggling behind her hands, which are held in an upright position, slightly away from her mouth, with the palm facing her face.

Playing by the Local Rules: Eye Contact

In most Western countries, eye contact is a necessary ingredient for demonstrating respect, yet throughout much of Asia the opposite is true. When you give someone from the Far East what you think is an honest look in the eye, they interpret the gesture as rude, showing a lack of respect, and feel personally affronted.

When conversing with someone from the Far East, avoid making eye contact, except for an occasional glance to make sure that they're still there. Then, quickly avert your eyes again.

Always watch for how a person gestures. The manner in which the action is performed adds to the meaning of the gesture. Maria, for example, was working in Japan with a Japanese colleague, preparing a client presentation. She asked him if he was pleased with the work they had done together. He told her that, yes, he was. A couple of days later Maria heard through the grapevine that her colleague wasn't happy with the result and wanted to rework the presentation. When she asked him why he'd told her that it was all right when it wasn't, he replied: 'But I told you with sad eyes, Maria.'

In Nordic countries, Germany, and Great Britain, eye contact is important for demonstrating sincerity and trust. If you're ever invited to a Scandinavian's home for dinner, be prepared for some serious eye contact. After dinner, and often during the meal, your host raises her glass, looks you, and everyone else at the table directly in the eye, and says 'skoal'. Although the toast has its variations throughout the Nordic lands, the main point to remember is that direct and prolonged eye contact throughout the ritual is required.

I hold round-table discussions in the office for trainees to an international accountancy firm who represent many different cultures. Many Asian participants say that looking at a superior, or colleague, in the eye is difficult because that suggests arrogance and disrespect on the part of the younger person. On the other hand, global business culture expects eye contact, so they need to practise until they feel comfortable with eye contact. Conversely, if westerners are going to a culture where eye contact is restricted, they need to experience how it feels to create a relationship by averting their eyes, usually downward, with clients, superiors, and colleagues.

Inge and Jesper, friends from Denmark, invited us to their home for a long weekend. On Saturday night they hosted a formal dinner party for the four of us and ten other friends. Throughout the meal toasts were frequently made. Every time our generous and gracious host raised his glass he looked each guest directly in the eye as we raised our glasses in response. Not one of us failed to engage direct eye-to-eye contact with Inge and Jesper, as well as with the other guests at the table. Fortunately, we only toasted once during the serving of the hot food.

Part V
The Part of Tens

@RICHTENNANT

"I wouldn't read much into Mona's body language. She actually enjoys meeting new people."

In this part . . .

Every *For Dummies* book has a delicious and dainty group of chapters at the end of the book for you to consume with relish. Here you find ten tips for reading other people and ten tactics for improving your own silent communication skills. *Bon appetit*!

Chapter 13

Ten Ways to Find Out about Someone without Asking

So, you've seen someone who's caught your eye. Although she's interesting enough to investigate, you don't want to pump your friends for information at this stage. What do you do? Pay attention.

You have two eyes, two ears, and one mouth. Use them in that order and you may discover what qualities this person possesses that floats your boat or rings your bells, without you giving your game away.

Observing Eye Movements

Do they flash? Do they flicker? Are they dull and dreary? Turn to the eyes, the gateway to the soul, as your first point of reference.

No matter how much your mouth churns out information, your eyes reveal more. Eyes that turn downwards like Antonio Banderas's give the impression that the person is authoritative and caring. Women swoon at Banderas's combination of soulful eyes and strong physique. They also quiver at the new James Bond, Daniel Craig, he of the steely eyes and climbing-frame figure. What are that man's eyes saying?

Queen Elizabeth II seldom gives her emotions a public viewing, and quite right, too. Even though she shows a down-to-earth kindness in her eyes, they're covered by a gauze curtain to keep her feelings concealed from her public. Long live the Queen!

Princess Diana, on the other hand, drew her public in with her soulful eyes, averted looks, and vulnerable appearance. She was naturally skilled at creating empathy and captured the world's compassion by the tilt of her head and her upward gaze. Women today still copy this helpless and submissive pose that triggers nurturing reactions in most people if they're paying attention.

If the person in your sights returns your gaze with lowered eyelids, raised eyebrows, and slightly parted lips, she's showing you that she's interested in you and wants to take this further. How you choose to respond to that message is up to you.

For more on how to read eyes, head to Chapter 5.

Looking at Facial Expressions

By looking at the position of the mouth, the movement in the lips and what the nose is doing, you can quickly spot another person's happiness or pain, anger or despair, or just plain boredom. The most successful people in the public eye manipulate their facial expressions in order to elicit desired responses. They know what to show and when to show it.

The saying goes that behind every successful man is a strong woman. The best wives of accomplished men have a way of looking at their husband that raises his stature in the eyes of others. Their gaze is unwavering, full of attention, awe, and adoration. Former actress and second wife of President Ronald Regan, Nancy Reagan, was expert at influencing public opinion by the looks she showered upon her man. Like a love-struck teenager, she would gaze upon him with Bambi-like devotion. Her public displays of affection sent the message that Ronnie was a terrific guy.

At President Gerald Ford's funeral, his widow Betty, a highly respected and accomplished woman in her own right, showed the world how to behave with dignity and grace during times of loss, sadness, and public scrutiny. She didn't display a great outpouring of grief. At least, not openly. Television permitted you to see her lips quiver, her eyes moisten, and her occasional faltering step throughout the mourning period. You only had to look at her face to absorb both her pain and her fortitude.

Chapter 4 has details on the range of emotions that faces display.

Watching for Head Movements

Observe someone nodding in agreement, understanding, or with the desire to add her point of view to the speaker's. The eyes look engaged, the head is held upright, and her face is mobile. Slow nods tell you she's following the speaker, and fast nodding indicates a desire to jump into the conversation. A shake of the head tells you she's not buying the speaker's opinion.

Cocked, canted, and tilted heads tell you the other person's

- ✔ Thinking about what's going on
- ✔ Contemplating a retort
- ✔ Responding submissively

When you register head movements in combination with other gestures, such as lip and eye actions, you're better equipped to determine a person's attitude and its underlying message. Head to Chapter 3 for more on head movements.

Noticing Hand and Arm Gestures

Look at a person's hands for revealing gestures. If the fingers are tapping and the nails bitten, you can be sure she's filled with nervous anxiety. Someone flapping her hands like Prissy in *Gone With the Wind* is, well, in a flap!

When someone's hand goes to her mouth, you're safe in betting that she's holding back some kind of feeling, emotion, or attitude. And when her lips are firmly sealed, she's keeping her thoughts to herself.

Anyone rubbing her hands and licking her lips at the same time is feeling happy and excited, as long as the speed's up tempo. If the hand and lip rub is slow and deliberate, be careful. This person may be dreaming up a scheme, calculating her chances, or devising a strategy that benefits herself – and not you.

Arms crossed against the chest, hands tucked into the armpits or a lowered head and furrowed brow are not signs of a warm and welcoming person. Of course, she may just be reacting to a cold blast of air. Opened arms, a dropped-jaw smile, and an eyebrow flash conveys a sense of pleasure and excitement, whereas a pointed finger wagging in your face belongs to someone who's aggressive, controlling, and domineering. You may want to stay out of that person's way.

For more on hand and arm gestures, go to Chapters 7 and 8.

Observing Posture

An upright stance, with legs parallel and feet under knees, knees under hips, and hips under shoulders, marks out the strong and powerful individual. If her chest is thrust forward, with chin jutting out, and the jaw clenched, beware. She may have moved into aggressive territory.

Slumped shoulders, hands protecting the privates, and a downcast eye all indicate that the person's depressed or despondent. In a woman, crossed ankles and hands neatly folded in her lap suggest a prim and proper attitude, whereas men who sit with their legs splayed, their arms stretched across the back of their chair, and their chests pumped out, are showing how manly they are.

You can read more about posture in Chapter 6.

Considering Proximity and Orientation

Does a person get up close and personal when she's not been invited? Does she turn her back when you approach? You can tell a lot about a person's nature, attitude, and culture by the amount of space she places between the two of you, as well as how she positions her body in relation to yours.

If someone is feeling cooperative and helpful she sits next to you. If she's feeling competitive she sits across from you. If she really doesn't get on with you, she turns away.

Look at where a single person places herself in public places. Someone sitting with her back to the other people is clearly indicating that she wants no engagement with anyone, thank you very much. Although facing other people head on may indicate a fearless attitude, it can be a bit overwhelming for both the person assuming the position as well as other people. The person who sits at an angle is indicating that she is open to speaking with another person if the opportunity comes along.

Those with a sense of high status remain seated while others stand. People with a low sense of status hang back by the door when entering someone's office. Someone who believes she's of equal status with a colleague sits next to that person's desk.

Go to Chapter 9 for more information on the messages you send through positioning yourself in relation to others.

Paying Attention to Touching

Favourable judgement is most often given to the person who is able comfortably to touch someone else. Granted, Anglo-Saxons have more difficulty embracing the gesture, because their culture is one that refrains from touching. That small point aside, the people you see touching are the ones who are

- ✔ Offering information or advice
- ✔ Giving a command
- ✔ Making a request
- ✔ Persuading another person
- ✔ At a party
- ✔ Conveying enthusiasm
- ✔ Listening to another person's troubles
- ✔ In a dominant role

When another person touches you, that person is implying that a bond exists between the two of you. Unless, of course, that person's a politician, in which case you can figure she just wants your vote. Go to Chapter 8 for more on messages conveyed through touch.

Responding to Appearance

With some exceptions allowed for, the first impression you get of people comes through what you observe about their physical appearance. You may start by noticing their clothes. Clothes, as a reflection of the wearer, send out messages for others to interpret. They're a sign of what the person wearing them is like. If the person you're analysing wears clean, well fitting clothes, has had a recent hair cut, and brushes twice a day, you're looking at someone who has a sense of personal pride.

And what about fitness? Whatever the investment in clothing and accessories, without a fit body reflecting an active mind, a person has trouble convincing an observer that no confidence issues exist that aren't being addressed. To find out more about how confidence is reflected in the way you present yourself, take a look at *Building Self-Confidence For Dummies* by Kate Burton and Brinley Platts.

People who want to present themselves at the top of their game pay attention to their outward appearance. They know the impact the visual message has on people's opinion of them.

Checking Timing and Synchronisation

A skilful communicator knows the impact that time has on perceptions and relationships. Others may struggle with time and use it ineffectively, adversely affecting their ability to communicate.

In Western culture people place great importance on time. They value pace, punctuality, and a pre-determined schedule. The person who acts by this code is viewed positively. Europeans and North Americans find the concepts of tardiness, slowness, and unstructured time difficult to grasp, much less view in a positive light. If you want to keep your mother-in-law happy, show up on time.

In India, Saudi Arabia, and other far- and middle-eastern cultures, people have a more relaxed approach towards time. In these countries keeping people waiting for appointments and allowing interruptions during meetings is common. Doing so is not intended to be rude. Time is considered to be flexible and schedules are simply loose guidelines to work around.

When you're interacting comfortably with another person and have established a good rapport you may find that your body movements match one another's. Your gestures and actions harmonise while you both subconsciously copy or reflect the other person's actions. Your movements are coordinated, or synchronised. Like two dancers you're both moving to the same rhythm. Imagine the ensuing chaos if your movements were waltz-like while the person you're interacting with moved in time to the jitterbug. Figuratively speaking, you'd be bumping into and tripping over one another and your communication would suffer.

If you pay attention to the other person and match your body movements, your communication is going to be more effective. So, if you want to keep your father-in-law happy, get your body in sync with his. By nodding at his jokes, smiling at his stories, and recognising by the cant of his head that cocktail hour has begun, your body reflects and responds to the signals he's sending out. And that is going to make him feel good.

After listening to a long-winded conversation, the person who wants to make a point moves quite conspicuously when she thinks the speaker is about to come to a conclusion. Her body rhythm differs from the speaker's, indicating that she now wants to speak.

Scrutinising Non-verbal Aspects of Speech

Because we take meaning from the way a message is delivered as well as from the words themselves, it's advisable to pay attention to the non-verbal aspects of speech. The volume, the pitch, the pace, and the tone of a person's voice can give you a pretty good idea of someone's mood and attitude. Add in accent, rate, and emphasis and the picture becomes clearer.

You can usually tell a person's mood by the way she uses her voice. If the voice is low in volume, sombre in tone, slow in speed, and lacking in emphasis, you can figure that she's feeling sad or depressed. If the pitch is high, the pace quick, and the words tumble out of her mouth, chances are that she's in a state of excitement.

If a person lifts the pitch at the ends of her sentences and is neither asking a question nor Australian, you may be right in thinking she's feeling a bit insecure or uncertain about what she's saying.

Nervousness and deception, characterised by stuttering, stammering, or adding 'ums', 'ers', and 'ahs', indicate that someone's not clear about what she wants to say. Polished performers eliminate those space fillers and count on the pause to provide authority and indicate confidence.

Anyone who can make you laugh has got to be okay, right? Laughter is infectious. It makes you feel good. Laughter lifts the spirits and as long as you laugh with, rather than at, another person, the results are positive and beneficial.

Finally, the person who wants to demonstrate that she has higher status than another, aims to have the last word on a subject.

Chapter 14

Ten Ways to Improve Your Silent Communication

*I*f you've ever stood in awe of someone who's comfortable asking for what he wants, dresses in a way that you admire, and leaves people feeling good about themselves, now's your chance to discover the secrets. Actually, they're not such big secrets. It's more a matter of attitude. If you're aware of your current behaviour and are willing to do what you have to do to get the results you want, you're well on your way to achieving them.

Taking an Interest

The best communicators take an interest in other people. They can empathise with you, and just by looking at you, know how you're feeling. Think about those people whose company you thoroughly enjoy. I'm willing to bet – and I'm not a betting woman – that the ones whose company you seek out are the ones who make you feel good about yourself.

If you think you're a good communicator but for some odd reason no one's seeking out your company, perhaps the problem is that you're so busy focusing on yourself and your interests that you're failing to notice other people, what they're saying, and how they're behaving.

I once described another person as 'boring'. The friend I was speaking to admonished me by suggesting that if I think someone is 'boring' I should think about that person for five minutes, and if I still think he's boring, I should think about him for another five minutes, and continue to do so until I find something about that person that I find interesting. He also suggested that I may want to consider my own behaviour. Was I acting in a way that brought out the best in the other person? Was I demonstrating an interest in the person, or was I focusing only on myself and my own interests?

Knowing What You Want to Express

A clearly formulated thought, simply expressed and without apology, makes life so much easier for both the speaker and the listener. Instead of umming, erring, or ahhing, the expert communicator leaves those space fillers to the people who are afraid to state their beliefs and hesitant about saying what they feel.

Before speaking, whether stating an opinion or asking a question, have your thoughts clearly formulated in your mind. If you're speaking as you're thinking about what you want to say, you may have to make several attempts before you get your words out the way you want them to be heard. By then your listeners and observers may have departed.

Modelling Excellence

Every so often you meet someone who has the knack for communicating in such a way that keeps you hanging onto his every word and makes you long to be in his company. That's the person whose behaviour you want to model.

Observing other people gives you the chance to see what works and what doesn't. If someone uses body language that's inclusive and encompassing, and open and welcoming, you're going to feel comfortable in his company. If someone presents himself in such a way that commands your attention and elicits your respect, you sit up and take notice.

Deciding what you consider to be excellent behaviour requires that you establish your standards. Review your current behaviour and acknowledge where you may have some blind spots. Concede that some of your behaviour may put people off. By recognising what you do well and where there's room for improvement you give yourself a foundation to build on. By following the examples of people whose behaviour produces the kind of results you aspire to, you have, in effect, a template to follow.

Mirroring Others

By mirroring, or reflecting the behaviour of another person, you can create a natural rapport that leads to effective communication. Mirroring the behaviour of another person tells him that what he's doing is acceptable in the context of your interaction. Mirroring demonstrates that you're willing to echo what you're observing in order to create an environment where both you and the other person can communicate freely and comfortably.

Once you have matched the other person's behaviour you can then take the lead yourself and get him to mirror yours. For tips and techniques for effective mirroring techniques, head to Chapter 1. I also recommend *Neuro-linguistic Programming For Dummies* by Romilla Ready and Kate Burton.

Practising Gestures

Some people struggle when it comes to using appropriate gestures to express themselves effectively. Smiling, opening their arms, and standing upright just doesn't sit comfortably with them. One person I know, who's a thoroughly pleasant fellow, habitually frowns, making him look angry and out of sorts. He wasn't aware that he had this habit until someone pointed it out to him. His genuine interest in other people means that he really concentrates on what they do and say, causing his brow to furrow. He thought he was showing interest. Other people thought he was showing disapproval.

If you want to project a specific image or attitude you may need to practise the appropriate gestures until they become a natural part of your behavioural repertoire. It may feel uncomfortable at first, as any new habit does. The more you practise the more at ease you feel and the gestures become second nature.

Developing Timing and Synchronisation

How people relate to time is central to who they are. In Western cultures people are obsessed with time and place a high value on punctuality and keeping to a pre-determined schedule. They consider keeping another person waiting to be rude and hostile.

If you want to impress others in such a culture, fill your time with meetings, appointments, and activities. Moving and working at a fast pace earns you more respect than if you move at a slower tempo. Slowness is equated to laziness, although someone who takes a more measured approach towards time may actually accomplish more than those people who dash about, often accomplishing little or nothing.

One way you can improve your use of time is to anticipate what's coming next. Before completing one task, think about what may follow, and plan your approach. This anticipatory scanning technique is particularly useful for anyone working with the public, such as waiters and airline personnel. A skilled employee anticipates the customers' needs in advance by identifying cues and specific signals, and responds to them before being asked.

Sometimes you feel good and can communicate with ease and enthusiasm. At other times, all you want to do is turn out the lights and pull the covers over your head. The body's natural time rhythms influence these moods. When the rhythms become disrupted as happens when you're suffering from jet lag or too many late nights, you may find yourself making mistakes and behaving irrationally. Go get yourself a good night's sleep and see how you do in the morning.

If you want to show that you're paying attention to a person who's speaking, synchronise your body movements with his. It has been argued that by having your gestures echo those of others, a rhythmic pattern is produced that enhances communication.

Dressing the Part

Glad rags, jeans, or a pinstriped suit? What's it to be? It depends on how you want to be perceived and the impression you want to make. The way you dress sends out messages about you. Observe how your friends and colleagues present themselves and adapt your style to meet theirs.

The key is knowing what's expected and what's acceptable. If you work for a traditional organisation where a suit and tie for men and jackets and skirts or trousers for women are the norm, you're tempting fate to show up in tracksuit trousers and a hoodie. To do so makes other people uncomfortable. They would also question your judgement.

Sure, you want to be comfortable and dress in a way that reflects who you are. You also want to be appropriate. You really do. Your clothes needn't be expensive. They do need to be clean, in good repair, and suited to your shape and style. They need to represent you at your best and make the people you're with feel comfortable.

Acting the Way You Want to Be Perceived

First, you decide how you want to be perceived. Then, you behave in a way that creates that impression.

You may never have thought about the way you act, thinking that how you behave is just fine. And it probably is, most of the time. Just remember, if you want to be perceived in a certain way you have to give some thought to your behaviour. If you want people to think that you're the life and soul of the party you smile, laugh, and make an effort to put other people at their ease. If you want to be taken seriously, your actions need to be more contained, and your facial expression more sober. The trick is to determine how you want people to perceive you, and after that, to take on the behaviour of that kind of person.

Demonstrating Awareness

Some people just don't get it. They seem to be blind to their own behaviour and the impact it has on others. If you pay attention to the reactions of other people you develop an awareness of what works when and where.

You may say that what other people think about you doesn't matter. And in many ways you're right. Yet at particular times someone's opinion of you can matter very much. By knowing how certain people respond to specific behaviours, you can adapt your style to meet theirs thus creating an environment that's conducive to successful communication.

In addition to focusing on your own behaviour, observe how other people behave. By paying attention to how someone else is conducting himself you can respond in a way that makes that person feel noticed and valued. And if you make someone feel that he matters, you're going to matter very much to him.

Asking for Feedback

It doesn't hurt, well, not too much, to ask how people perceive you. If their response matches your vision of yourself, all's well. If, however, they tell you one thing and you thought you were projecting something else, you may want to spend some time re-evaluating your perceptions.

When you ask for feedback, be specific. Otherwise you leave the door open for all kinds of information to come flooding through, some of which may not be pertinent or helpful. By getting honest reactions to your behaviour you can continue what's working well and adjust what's not, in order to assure that you communicate accurately and that your actions support your message.

Make sure that you're open and receptive to the feedback you get and that you listen attentively. If you don't, the person responding may get exasperated and walk away, leaving you none the wiser. If you don't understand, ask for clarification. Respect and acknowledge the other person's point of view. This doesn't mean that you have to agree with what he's saying, just that you value and allow him his observations. Finally, thank him for his opinions. After all, you asked for them.

Index

FOR DUMMIES®

Making Everything Easier!™

Portable Editions

978-1-119-97437-6   978-1-119-97440-6   978-1-119-97436-9   978-1-119-97431-4   978-1-119-97445-1

978-1-119-97439-0   978-1-119-97442-0   978-1-119-97444-4   978-1-119-97434-5

1-119-97435-2   978-1-119-97441-3   978-1-119-97438-3   978-1-119-97443-7   978-1-119-97446-8

978-1-119-97432-1   978-1-119-97433-8   978-0-470-01903-0   978-0-470-77765-7

For more information call +44 (0) 1243 843291

11-34874

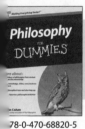

FOR DUMMIES®

The easy way to get more done and have more fun